✳ wedding duties for men

essentials

carole chapman
& wendy hobson

foulsham
LONDON • NEW YORK • TORONTO • SYDNEY

foulsham

The Publishing House, Bennetts Close, Cippenham, Slough,
Berkshire, SL1 5AP, England

ISBN 0-572-02761-3

Printed in Great Britain by Cox & Wyman, Reading, Berkshire

Contents

Introduction

You are going to be one of the most important men at a wedding – perhaps the groom, the best man, the bride's or groom's father, or an usher. Whatever your role, you'll need to know how you fit into the bigger picture: what's expected of you, what your duties are, where you are meant to be when, and what you are supposed to be doing. Apart from anything else, you are far more likely to enjoy the whole proceedings if you aren't constantly worrying that you are going to do or say something that will mess up the whole thing and make you look a fool!

So why should men need a separate book? You're probably having trouble just staying interested in all the detailed planning that the bride and her mother (plus all their best friends and every other woman involved in the wedding) have been immersed in for the last few months. You may have tried really hard to care about the colour of the bridesmaids' accessories or whether stephanotis or gypsophila would be more appropriate for the bouquet (what?!) but, let's face it, you're not really into that kind of detail. However, you do have a huge contribution to make and you want to be a vital part of the process. You want to know what you need to do, and how to do it well. And that's what this book is all about. It will give you all the facts you need without the unnecessary trimmings. It will help you to understand what's going on so that you can offer advice and support, and it will tell you what everyone (including you) is responsible for, so the whole process can go like clockwork.

Whether the wedding is to be a small register office service followed by a cosy lunch for your closest friends or a full-blown traditional church pageant with all the regalia and a lavish banquet, this book is for you. Size, as they say, doesn't matter. Since every wedding is different, you can simply personalise the book by deleting the things that don't apply to you. Then you just fill in the personal diaries to make the book your unique handbook with all the facts and figures at your fingertips.

Whatever the style of the wedding, everyone wants it to be a day to remember. In most wedding plans, the bride and her mother are the key players – they are the ones who call the shots. Your first task is to get involved as early as you can so that you can have your say, because that's when the groundwork is set. The groom who sits back and lets things happen will find a chamber orchestra at the reception when he would have preferred a rock band. And the bride's father who leaves all the decisions to the girls will probably find himself with a far larger bill than he ever envisaged. Once everything is booked, you've missed your chance, so remember, communication is vital. (That, by the way, is just the first of many tips for being that one-in-a-million guy and earning some brownie points. There are plenty more in the book – watch out for the ☺.)

The bride and her mother will be doing a thousand and one things before the big day – choosing the bridesmaids, buying the dresses, working out guest and gift lists, sending invitations, doing table plans and booking everyone from the photographer to the florist – and that's just the start. So, here's brownie-point ☺ tip number two. Don't be surprised when (and it will be 'when', not 'if') she gets stressed – anticipate it and have a bottle of wine or a beautifully wrapped bottle of lavender bath foam (very relaxing – remember that) in the glove box of the car to bring out at just the right moment when things look set to come unravelled. Be supportive, not dismissive. It's not difficult but – as the crows so famously said in *Dumbo:* 'You've got to use a little 'cology'!

This book contains everything for every man who has an important part to play at a wedding. So whether you want to be the best groom, the best best man, the best father or the best usher, read through everything to get the overall picture. Then focus on your specific section so you'll be relaxed, efficient and, well, simply the best, on the day.

Don't forget to look out for:
☺ Neat tips to get you in everyone's good books
✄£ Tips that can save money without sacrificing style or fun
➤ General tips and also pitfalls to avoid!

Chapter 1
The Groom

You are the man of the hour! You have met the girl of your dreams and you are going to spend the rest of your lives together. It's exciting, and more than a little worrying – but relax. You can do it, and you can enjoy it. It's all about attitude. You want to be involved and to have an impact so that your day of celebration really belongs to you and your partner, but let's be honest, you probably don't want to be involved in every aspect of the planning. So the first thing you need to do is to think about what is really important to you and what is not. Be there with opinions, support and constructive comments when it matters to you; take a back seat when it doesn't. That way you won't get bogged down and you'll keep your focus.

In this chapter, you'll find everything you need to know about the planning, the organisation and the big day itself. Read it through, personalise it to suit your circumstances, and you'll be ready to be the star of the show – second to the bride, of course (but you'll get used to that).

First things first

A proposal can be a spur-of-the-moment thing, but that's not the norm. Even though there is usually a specific proposal and engagement, most couples work up to it gradually, thinking about and talking through the implications before the actual event. Since it's such an important step, that makes good sense. Love is crucial, of course, but a lasting relationship takes hard work and has to withstand the realities of life. I can leave the love bit to you – you have found the girl of your dreams and you want to spend the rest of your life with her. But here are a few ideas on more prosaic things you should have been thinking about and talking through with your partner either before the engagement or soon after.

Am I free to marry anyone?
No.

- You must have been born male and your partner female.
- Both of you must not be already married to a living spouse or going through a divorce.
- Both of you must be of sound mind and act by your own consent. Which, put in plain English, means that you must know what you're doing.
- Both of you must be over 16 (England, Wales and Scotland).
- If either of you is under 18 and is marrying for the first time, you must have your parents' or legal guardians' consent (England and Wales).

- You may not marry your:
  - Mother, adoptive mother/former adoptive mother
  - Daughter, adoptive daughter/former adoptive daughter
  - Father's mother
  - Mother's mother
  - Son's daughter
  - Daughter's daughter
  - Sister
  - Father's sister
  - Mother's sister
  - Wife's mother
  - Wife's daughter
  - Father's wife
  - Son's wife
  - Father's father's wife
  - Mother's father's wife
  - Wife's father's mother
  - Wife's mother's mother
  - Wife's son's daughter
  - Wife's daughter's daughter
  - Son's son's wife
  - Daughter's son's wife
  - Brother's daughter
  - Sister's daughter

Brother and sister include half-brother and half-sister.

What's life together going to be like?

It's a good idea to try to visualise what life will be like with your partner. You should by now be asking yourself a few questions.

- Where will you live?
- Will your work commitments have a major impact on your home life? For example, does one of you travel a lot or do shift work?
- What about her annoying habits? Can you learn to live with them?
- Are you used to your own space? How can you make sure you both have enough time on your own or with friends?
- Do you expect your partner to go out with her friends on a regular basis?
- Do you expect to carry on your existing hobbies, even if they are very time-consuming?
- Do you have a good sex life? Or, if you have decided to wait until after marriage, have you discussed your expectations?

> ➤ You can't change other people. You can change yourself but only if you really want to. Learn about compromise, and about having equal respect for your own and your partner's opinions. That will mean sometimes you'll need to stand your ground, and sometimes you'll have to do things you don't especially like.

What about finances?

When you are in love, money may not seem that important, but unfortunately it can and does come between couples who might otherwise have a good relationship. Take some time to calculate your joint income and expenditure and establish how you are going to manage your money in the immediate future, and how you would feel about things if circumstances were to change. Above all, be realistic.

- Do you earn similar salaries?
- Will you have a joint or separate bank accounts?
- If they are to be separate, how will you share your living costs?
- What if one partner has a much higher salary than the other?
- How would you feel about your wife earning more than you?
- Is one of you a spendthrift?
- Is either of you in debt?
- What would happen if one of you lost their job?
- Is one of you better at managing money than the other?
- Are you planning to take out a mortgage?
- How do you both feel about saving?
- Does either of you have a pension? If not, are you going to start one?
- How much do you think you should spend on holidays and entertainment? What are your spending priorities?

- Fill in the Household income and expenditure checklists (see page 116) and assess your future spending power.

What about children?

Most couples don't want to start a family straight away, but having children is a life-changing experience, and one that lasts a lifetime, so think carefully about your views on starting a family. Your attitudes will almost certainly change as time passes, but it's not a good idea to start out at opposing ends of the spectrum.

- Do you both want children, or does only one – or neither – of you?
- How long do you want to wait before starting a family?
- How many children would you like?
- Do you expect your wife to take the major responsibility for childcare?
- How would you feel if your wife wanted to return to work full time?
- What if you found you could not have children?

One of you may have children from a previous relationship, and obviously it is crucial that you take them into your considerations.

- Will they live with you?
- What are the arrangements with the other parent for contact, parental responsibility, and so on?

13

- What about their maintenance costs?
- How do they feel about you getting married?
- Do they get on well with both you and your new partner?

Where are we going to live?

You may have to live with your parents for a time, or you may be renting or buying a house or an apartment. In any event, you need to think through the options and decide what you want, what you can afford, and what you can achieve. Remember that whatever you decide, it's not for ever.

Home	Advantages	Disadvantages
Buying	Your home should be a long-term investment	It is an expensive commitment and you will need a deposit
Renting	You don't need a hefty deposit; it's more flexible	There's no return on your money; it may not be much cheaper than a mortgage
Sharing with family, friends, colleagues or acquaintances	It's a shared financial responsibility	There's little privacy and it's not much like being married

If you intend to move into a property you haven't previously shared, begin home-hunting as soon as you can, particularly if you're planning to buy. Home-buying is a notoriously lengthy process, littered with all kinds of legalities and delays and, whether you are buying or renting, just finding the right place can take months. So make an early start to give yourselves the best chance of finding exactly what you want and avoid the horrors of a last-minute hitch.

What insurance will we need?

Somehow thinking about insurance doesn't top the list of things to do at this, the most romantic time of your life. But it's well worth spending a little time on it now – it could save you a lot of time, trouble and money later.

Life insurance: You may be covered for personal insurance under your mortgage but if not, arrange life insurance in each other's favour because if one of your two incomes ceases, the working partner could be in financial difficulty. If you plan a family, this is especially important.

Buildings insurance: This is obligatory if you buy your home.

✂£ It is usually cheaper to arrange buildings insurance independently rather than through your mortgage provider. If you do take out the insurance with your mortgage provider, you can change it later if you wish.

Home contents insurance: Secure your home contents against loss such as from theft and fire. As time passes, you can increase the cover every year or so to reflect your additional assets.

✂£ Some insurance companies offer a discount if you take out more than one insurance policy with them.

The engagement

An engagement usually lasts from about six months to a couple of years. It's meant to be the time not only to make the wedding plans and arrangements for your new life together, but also to allow the two sides of what will be your new family to get used to one another.

☺ It used to be traditional to commemorate an engagement with a portrait photo of you and your fiancée and it still goes down a treat with the parents. Whether you frame a nice photo taken by a friend, or opt for a professional portrait, they will love it.

When and where do I pop the question?

Things may have changed, but not that much – it is still the custom for the man to pop the question, even in leap years. It's a special moment, so it's up to you to make it really special.

☺ You don't have to understand why, but most women like a little romance. So don't abandon the soft lights, Belgian chocolates and expensive champagne (no Milk Tray and own-label cava, please) just because you think it's cheesy. If you are doing something because you want to make your partner happy, it's not insincere. And if you make her happy, that should make you happy. Jackpot – a win/win situation.

Think about what would make it perfect for both of you. If your girlfriend hates surprises – and some people do – try dropping some subtle hints to give her a clue. If she's a romantic, go for the candle-lit dinner, champagne and roses. If she's adventurous, you could book a balloon flight and pop the question as you float across the countryside. If she's a real thrill freak, take her bungee-jumping and drop down on one knee just before you leave the platform. Be different.

✄£ If you can't afford two dozen red roses – and let's face it, who can? – don't buy a cheap mixed bunch of flowers from your local garage. Go for a single, long-stemmed red rose or a tiny, beautifully wrapped box of continental chocolates. Style is what matters.

What type of engagement ring should I buy?

A gold ring with one or more diamonds is probably the most popular choice but it's entirely a matter of personal preference. One thing is sure: the days when a man produced a ring and placed it on his girlfriend's finger when he proposed are virtually over; nowadays it's usual to choose the ring together. If you happen to have a family ring that you want her to wear, you might want to put out 'feelers' about this first, just in case she is not happy with the idea.

☺ Your fiancée will probably wear her engagement ring every day for the rest of her life, so it's not unreasonable for her to want to choose it herself.

Think about what you can reasonably afford. If money is no object, a month's salary is considered a normal outlay for an engagement ring, but you may not have that kind of money to spare, or you may have other priorities: the wedding itself, the deposit on a house, the honeymoon. Set a realistic budget that you both agree before you leave for the shops, tell the jeweller your upper limit and stick to it.

☺ The jeweller will probably show you a few rings that are just above your price limit. Be prepared for this and adjust the price you tell him accordingly.

Apart from the traditional diamond engagement ring, there are many alternatives, including a family ring or heirloom and antique rings. Birthstones are also a popular choice as their various stones are said to symbolise particular qualities. Some women think it lucky to have their fiancé's birthstone rather than their own.

Month	Birthstone	Meaning
January	Garnet	Constancy
February	Amethyst	Sincerity
March	Bloodstone	Courage
April	Diamond	Innocence
May	Emerald	Success
June	Pearl	Health
July	Ruby	Love
August	Sardonyx	Married happiness
September	Sapphire	Wisdom
October	Opal	Hope
November	Topaz	Fidelity
December	Turquoise	Harmony

➤ Superstition says it's unlucky to buy the engagement and wedding rings on the same day.

Should I expect an engagement gift from my fiancée?

It's unusual for men to wear engagement rings. However, many women like to give a gift in return to mark this very special occasion; something permanent is the norm. Drop some hints if you like – a gold signet ring, gold chain, tie clip, cufflinks or a watch are all suitable – but don't forget the forthcoming major outlay you both face.

Who should be the first to know?

Although you may be eager to tell your friends the good news, traditionally both sets of parents should be the first to find out (tell the bride's before the groom's). Of course, if you have children, then they should be the first to know and it's obviously vital that they feel secure and comfortable about their future.

☺ Although the chances are that your fiancée's father won't expect you to abide by tradition and ask for his consent, it's still one of the best ways of establishing a good son-in-law/father-in-law relationship and will earn you many brownie points – if he's happy about the situation, of course.

Once the parents know, the general announcement may be reserved for a special party to mark the engagement (see page 22). Failing that, pick up the phone, write some letters or send some e-mails. Try to make sure you tell the important people directly. Your favourite aunt won't be too pleased if she learns the happy news in the queue at the post office.

Your fiancée's parents will probably put an announcement in their local paper. If you live in different towns, you or your mum might like to put one in your local.

When should we introduce the parents to each other?

It's a good idea to introduce the sets of parents early on so they'll feel more relaxed in each other's company by the big day. Choose a location that will put everyone at ease: an informal supper, a chat over a pint at the local, whatever you think they will prefer. The venue doesn't matter as long as no one feels out of place. Traditionally your parents host the evening and pay for it (stemming from the tradition that the bride's parents will be paying for the wedding).

Use the occasion to discuss the type of wedding you'd both like and make sure everyone is happy with the implications. Think about the timing, the place and the scale of the event. Consider whether a number of guests would have to travel long distances. Get a feel for the whole day.

One of the most important things to discuss is how your ideal plans translate into pounds sterling. The cost of an average wedding is over £8,000 (turn-of-the-century prices) so let that thought sink in before you agree to all the trimmings. Talk about who is contributing and make sure that what you are planning is within the families' financial reach. If your fiancée's parents think they are paying for one-third of the expenses and then discover, once the planning is well under way, that you expect them to foot the whole bill, it's not going to make for a good start with your in-laws!

One way to keep control of spending is to establish early on what are your top priorities – the things you can't do without. Then add to these, according to the money you have available. You really don't have to break the bank; it is possible to have a wonderful day without eating into your parents' retirement funds.

> ➤ Most people are embarrassed to talk about money. Get over it! Start talking early and make everything clear – everyone will feel much better for it.

If a meeting is impossible, perhaps because of distance, your mum traditionally writes to your fiancée's parents on behalf of herself and your dad, expressing their happiness at the news and saying that they're looking forward to meeting at the wedding. With letters, telephones, e-mails, video e-mails and even text messaging to choose from, there's no excuse for the parents not to communicate, even across continents.

What happens at an engagement party?

You don't have to have an engagement party, but it's a good excuse for a celebration. The traditional route is that the bride's parents throw a party for friends and relatives, during which her father makes the announcement and toasts the happy couple. The groom replies by proposing the health of both sets of parents. Your fiancée will no doubt be eager to show off her engagement ring but it's not usually worn in public until the engagement has been officially announced.

> ➤ You'll want the whole world to know, but **don't** make the announcement at someone else's wedding – that's their special day, not yours!

One small, fine point of etiquette for your guests: it is correct to congratulate the groom (you), but your fiancée should be wished 'much future happiness', since congratulating her implies that she was successful in 'capturing' you! Guests are not expected to bring gifts, although they probably will do so as soon as they hear the news.

> ✄£ You don't have to have an engagement party. You can keep it to a few drinks with friends and close family.

What if the engagement is then broken off?
If your fiancée breaks off the engagement, she should offer to return the ring and any gifts you've bought her. It's your decision whether you take them back. However, if you're the

one who breaks it off, she's entitled to keep the ring and any gifts you have given her. If the engagement ring was a family heirloom or your mum's engagement ring, then obviously you'll want that back, so you'll have to explain that to her.

It is essential to let people know that the engagement has been broken off if you have already set a date for the wedding. Even if you haven't, it is probably a good idea to make some sort of announcement anyway. Your fiancée should be the first to announce the broken engagement. The traditional way was to put a notice in the papers, but since few sets of relatives and friends are likely to read the same local paper these days, it is probably more likely that you will have to telephone or drop people a line. There's no need to explain the reasons. Engagement gifts from other people must be returned to their donors.

What happens next?

Whether on bended knee after a lavish candle-lit dinner for two or on the dance floor at the local disco, her answer was 'I will' or 'Yes'. So, congratulations – this is it! You've braved your future father-in-law and got his blessing, you've introduced the sets of parents and laid the groundwork for the sort of occasion you would like your wedding to be. So far, so good. But if you think you can now rest on your laurels until the big day and let your fiancée and her mother do the rest, think again! (Actually, you can – and some men do – but it is a seriously bad idea.

For a start, just think of all those opportunities for spending **your** money . . .)

How will I be involved in the wedding arrangements?

Your fiancée and her mother will be the key players in the organisation, but you have a crucial role too. The fact that your perspective on what is important may be different from theirs doesn't mean it's any less valid. You need to work together so that everyone is happy – and that's good practice for marriage. Join in the discussions, express your opinion, defer to your fiancée's better judgement when it's appropriate. Keep abreast of what's going on, and when you know it's really important to her or she'll do a far better job than you ever could, then just smile and nod your approval. When it's something that really matters to you, or it's a job she hates, or you know you can get it done in half the time, that's the time for you to be there with a constructive opinion, support and offers of help.

> ➤ If something is important to you, say so. Be tactful but be honest. Now is a good time to learn that very few people can read their partners' minds.

It'll soon become obvious that your fiancée and her mother will be very busy and the sooner they start planning the better. They'll need good advice on all aspects from the practical to the fanciful, so suggest your fiancée buys a good comprehensive book on weddings or buy one for her – see the list in our Wedding Collection on page 250.

Although much of the decision-making and organisation may not traditionally involve you, good communication with your fiancée and her mother is essential if the planning and preparations are to go without a hitch, so make it clear that you expect to be consulted on most issues. They may actually want you to be very much involved or they may be happy for you to sit back and leave it all to them. Whichever it is, it's vital that you make your preferences known and be supportive even if you may not be taking a very active part in the preparations. Talk about all of the options for all the decisions: the venues, the size of the guest list, how much you're able to spend, the attendants and clothes. If you've got any particular ideas, air them as soon as you can – even if you're not able to take them up, at least you'll never think, 'I wish I'd asked if she'd like to . . . '.

➤ Language is a powerful thing, so be careful how you use it. For example, 'I don't care; do whatever you like' is a definite no-no. Be cautious with: 'I'll be happy with whatever you choose', and 'But you'll do it so much better than I do' – they both sound perilously like 'I couldn't give a toss as long as I don't have to do it'. If you are given a choice, express your preference honestly. If the answer is 'I like this one slightly better but I'd be happy with either', say so.

How do we set the date?

It's virtually impossible to arrange a formal wedding in less than six weeks. A realistic minimum period of engagement is three months, but it's better if you've six months to plan, especially for a traditional church bash. Talk through the options with your fiancée and you may find that the restrictions on your time choose the date for you!

➤ Superstition says that it's unlucky to marry on the bride's birthday, but particularly lucky if husband and wife share the same birthday, though they should be a year or two apart.

When setting the date, consider these questions.

- Can you both have time off work for the wedding and honeymoon?
- Do you want the wedding to coincide with your annual holiday?
- Does either of you have any business trips planned?
- If so, could you extend one in order to save money on your honeymoon travel expenses?
- Do you particularly want a spring, summer, autumn or winter wedding?
- Do you want to take advantage of off-season honeymoon discounts?
- When are both sets of parents free?
- Are there regular dates when either set of parents goes away?

- When are all your closest friends free?
- Have you considered a weekday wedding? If you do go for this option, will your wedding party and guests be able to attend?
- Will you have to book overnight accommodation for guests?
- Have you allowed enough time to plan everything?
- How long will it take to have the bride's dress made?
- Will you have time to save enough money?
- When are the church and reception venues you want available?
- If you have a particular date in mind, does it coincide with the local carnival or marathon or any other event that may cause problems with traffic, accommodation, etc?

Select and inform your wedding party members of your plans as early as possible so they don't book their annual holiday to clash with the wedding day.

✂£ Book your venues early – the most reasonably priced venues and services are booked up a long time in advance.

Are there any times we can't marry?

Marriages must, by law, take place between 8 am and 6 pm. The only exceptions are Jewish and Quaker ceremonies performed under special licence or a Registrar General's licence. Weddings can take place on any day except Christmas Day and Good

Friday. Weddings are not generally allowed in churches on Sundays or in synagogues on the Jewish Sabbath.

> ✀£ You can plan to marry on a weekday if you wish, but check that your wedding party members and guests will still be able to attend.

Who can marry us and where can we marry?
A marriage must be solemnised by an authorised person: this means superintendent registrars and registrars; ordained ministers of the Church of England; authorised ministers of other religions.

The building must normally be registered for marriages: churches and register offices qualify, obviously, but nowadays the list of registered premises includes lots of hotels where you can have the ceremony, reception and everything else you need, all on one site.

Who pays the bills?
The bride's family make most of the arrangements and traditionally the bride's father is expected to pay for almost everything too. Fortunately for those with daughters, this practice is changing.

Talk with both sets of parents about the overall budget and how you are going to divide it between you. The checklists starting on page 119 show you who traditionally pays for everything, but you can change that to suit yourselves. Fill in guesstimates of the cost to start with, then refine them when you know the actual costs.

☺ Make sure everyone is clear about what they are expected to pay for. It's much better to risk an embarrassing moment early on than to find a huge unexpected bill at the end which no one considers to be their responsibility.

The groom's duties

There are some things that are traditionally considered to be the groom's responsibility. Of course, it's up to you and your fiancée how much you conform but this is what is likely to be expected.

What are my main duties?

Apart from the obvious – turn up and say 'I will' – these are your main jobs.

- Obtain and pay for the necessary legal documentation from the minister or registrar.
- Pay for the ceremony.
- Choose your best man and ushers. Make sure they know what they are expected to do and that they do it.

- Organise the outfits for the principal men and pay for them if they are being hired.
- Organise and pay for the honeymoon.
- Buy a wedding ring.
- Organise the transport to the church, from church to reception, and from reception to honeymoon. Your best man will help.
- Pay for the flowers for the bride and her attendants, and for the buttonholes and corsages.
- Deliver a speech.

Anything else?

All through the book we'll be talking about communication, co-ordination and support, and basically that's what your job entails. You may not be where the buck stops for most things, but your fiancée will expect you to be involved in the decision-making and offer your help where you can.

The ceremony

While the hosts – usually the bride's parents – have a say in the style of the reception (because they are paying for it), the ceremony is very much up to you and your fiancée. There are four options – church, registry office, registered premises or abroad.

> ➤ A marriage in Britain has to be a public declaration before two adult witnesses by two people of different sexes who fulfil all the legal requirements (being of sound mind, and so on). This means she can't lock the doors on you once she's got you there and anyone who wants to is allowed to attend!

Obviously a crucial decision is whether you want a civil or a religious ceremony. Since your wedding is an occasion to cement your relationship, you should talk through the options with your fiancée so you can decide on something that is right for both of you. It will also enable you to include those individual touches that will make your day unique. Whatever you decide, you'll need to sort out both the logistical and legal aspects.

A civil wedding

A civil ceremony usually takes place in a registry office. You may decide on a civil ceremony because you don't share the same religious beliefs, or because you have no fixed religious convictions, or because one of you is divorced – or you may just be strapped for cash.

A civil ceremony is much shorter than a church wedding – it takes about ten minutes – and must not include any religious elements. Registry offices will have facilities for only a limited number of guests. The tradition of the bride arriving with her father isn't always followed – sometimes the bride and groom arrive together – and the bride may wear a smart dress or suit, rather than a traditional wedding dress, so your own outfit will be less formal. Discuss this with your bride as she may still choose a traditional dress.

A civil ceremony at approved premises

You can also have a civil ceremony at one of the many approved premises, in which case you could also hold your reception there, which is a very convenient option for everyone. Venues include stately homes, historic buildings, castles, civic halls, hotels and other suitable premises – even boats if they are permanently moored. Despite what we see on American television, marriages in the UK cannot take place in the open air, in a marquee or any other temporary structure or on most forms of transport. A directory of registered premises in England and Wales can be bought from the Office for National Statistics (see page 247) and at the time of going to print lists about 3,000 venues. There's no need to live in the district in which the marriage is to take place.

A church ceremony

If you opt for a church wedding, it is likely to be a more elaborate affair, but it may mean anything from carriage and horses, morning suits, huge white dress and a battalion of bridesmaids to a small, very focused and personal but equally joyous occasion.

Although you can get married in any church if the minister agrees, it is usually the bride's parish church. The first step is to meet and talk with the minister, who will explain the meaning of marriage and what is expected of you if you wish to be married in his or her church. If you are not already regular church-goers, you will probably be expected to attend the church. In any event you will be asked to go to a series of meetings to discuss marriage and its commitments, and to go through what the vows mean and what actually happens in the service.

There are basically four versions of the service, all very similar but with slightly different wording. The only major difference is whether or not the bride promises to obey; needless to say, that's **her** choice.

☺ Don't make the mistake of thinking that trying to persuade your future wife to go for the 'obey' option is a subject for humour – not more than once, anyway. Just trust me on this one.

You'll also have to decide which psalm to sing, which hymns and readings to choose, and what the organist will play at the processional (when the bride comes in), while you are signing the register, and at the recessional (when you and the bride leave the church). Your fiancée will probably make the final choices, but you may want to put forward your own ideas.

> ☺ Try to encourage a choice of hymns that everyone knows. You'll get a much better atmosphere going in church if everyone is feeling relaxed and singing loudly, rather mouthing the words soundlessly to an unfamiliar tune.

You can also have extras like a choir, bell-ringers, a soloist who sings while you are signing the register, and so on – you can even choose who plays the organ, if you want. Quite often, there's a rehearsal for the whole wedding party a week or so before the wedding.

> ✄£ A church choir, bell-ringers, soloist, and so on, all add to the costs, so are areas where you could make savings.

If you are of different faiths, you can ask the officiating minister whether a minister of your own church can attend the wedding to give his blessing. This is usually welcomed.

> ➤ Although Psalm 23 ('The Lord Is My Shepherd') is one of the most popular, do think twice about whether 'Yea though I walk through the valley of the shadow of death' is an appropriate thought for a joyous celebration.

A service of blessing

Some people who cannot marry in church – perhaps because one of them is divorced, or for other reasons – have a civil wedding followed by a church service of blessing as a religious acknowledgement of the marriage. You will need to discuss this option with the minister of your church.

Getting married abroad

Marrying abroad is becoming a very popular option, with holiday destinations such as the Caribbean proving to be firm favourites. If you marry abroad, you must fulfil the legal requirements both of Britain and of the country in which you'll marry. Contact a travel agency that specialises in overseas wedding packages and they'll handle everything for you. If you do it yourself, you must consult the relevant consulates and embassies. You can always have a religious service of blessing when you return home and a celebration party for those who didn't attend the wedding.

Who do we ask to be witnesses?
The law requires that you have two adult witnesses who sign the register. It's usual to ask the two fathers, or your best man and the chief bridesmaid, but the choice is up to you.

☺ Make sure you ask your chosen witnesses in advance, to ensure there's no confusion – you don't want a queue of people lining up to sign on the dotted line!

I'm marrying a foreigner – what's the first step?
If your fiancée is not British and is coming to this country to marry you, this is more complicated. Visit a solicitor and the relevant consulate or embassy so you can resolve questions about:
- Change of nationality.
- Domicile.
- Work permits.
- Position of spouses and children in the foreign national's country.
- Consequences of divorce.

The legal stuff

Marriage is a legal contract, so there are some hoops you have to jump through before you tie the knot. Here are the basics that you need to know. You'll find the relevant local contact numbers in your telephone book or Yellow Pages, and there is a list of national contact numbers on pages 247–48.

Basically, you'll find that there's a time lapse between applying for permission and that permission being granted. That's to allow anyone to object, and to make sure you are who you say you are and you have the right to be married.

☺ Don't leave everything to the last minute. Once you have set the date for the wedding, make a note in your diary when you should get the certificate, then do it!

Superintendent registrar's authority

This is the method you use if you have chosen a civil wedding. You need to fill in the forms obtained from the local register office (names, addresses, ages, etc.) and sign a declaration that there is no legal objection to the marriage.

You need to have lived in any district in England or Wales for at least seven days. Both of you must give notice to the superintendent registrar of that district. The authority will be issued to you 16 days after you have given formal notice, and then the marriage can take place within 12 months of the day you give notice.

> ➤ You'll need your original birth certificates for the registrar or minister and, if you have been married before, original documents proving that you are divorced or your former partner has died.

Banns

For a church ceremony, the minister has the legal authority to undertake the marriage, in the same way as a registrar. Instead of issuing a licence, he publishes the banns – which means that he reads out your names in church to tell everyone you intend to marry – at three Sunday services before the ceremony. If you live in different parishes, the banns have to be read in both parishes. You'll organise all this when you go to meet the minister who will be officiating at the service and you'll need to liaise with a second minister if you live in different parishes. Once the banns have been read, the ceremony must take place within three months.

> ☺ You should attend the church service to hear the banns read at least once.

Special circumstances

If you are skipping the planning process and going for a quick wedding, then you are unlikely to be reading this book. However, there are swifter ways of getting married, which are used in exceptional circumstances, for example in the case of one partner being seriously ill. You may obtain a superintendent registrar's certificate and licence, from – what a surprise – the superintendent registrar (see page 247). Alternatively, you can obtain a common or ecclesiastical licence from the Faculty Office in London (see page 248) or from the Bishop's Register Office in any cathedral city or from one of the Surrogates for granting licences in the diocese.

Getting married in Scotland or Northern Ireland

If one of you is resident in Scotland or Northern Ireland, you both apply to your local registrar in the usual way, as notices issued in Scotland or Northern Ireland are valid in England and Wales, and vice versa.

To marry in Scotland, you have to fill in a marriage notice, which you obtain from the local registrar, and he or she will prepare a marriage schedule. If you are to be married in a church or a different register office, you collect the schedule not more than a week before the wedding. Once signed by the couple, the witnesses and the minister, it has to be returned within three days of the ceremony.

The system in Northern Ireland is basically the same as the system in England and Wales, as you apply to the district registrar for the area in which you have lived for at least the last seven days. You can get the full information on all of this from the relevant General Register Office (see pages 247–48).

The wedding party and the guests

The 'wedding party' means you and your bride, the parents, and some specially chosen best friends. The original idea was that a bunch of the groom's mates distracted the bride's family while he whisked her off to be married, then the best man was sent back to her father to soothe tempers and negotiate terms for her dowry, etc. The idea of bridesmaids arose because the bride was considered to need friends around her for comfort and support in her new situation. They all dressed alike, which also handily confused any evil spirits who happened to be searching for a bride on whom to vent their ill-will. In early Roman times, the wedding party also protected the couple's money during the wedding celebrations!

Use the listing for the wedding party on page 106 to keep a note of all the names and phones numbers.

☺ You are likely to make some long-standing friends among your young male relatives if you persuade the bride that something a bit more modern than velvet breeches and frilled shirts would suit the pageboys.

The bride will choose her bridesmaids, usually her sisters or close friends or perhaps your sister. If there are younger cousins or nieces, be careful to be seen to be fair about the choices. She might also choose a flower girl. She is usually the smallest of the bridesmaids, who walks ahead of the couple throwing flower petals in their path. If your fiancée is keen on the idea, make sure you check with the minister first. She may also opt for one or two pageboys.

☺ Most little girls would love to be a bridesmaid, so if you and your fiancée have a large number of younger sisters, small cousins, nieces, etc., the chances are there will be someone who will have to be left out and disappointed. Think of a special job for them to do on the day to make them feel special – their mothers will be eternally grateful. It could be handing out sweets or taking presents to the display table – it doesn't matter much. If you can't think of anything else to soothe hurt feelings, what about a mini-corsage for their dress?

How do I choose my best man?
Your best man will be your closest friend or your brother. Ask him in good time and make sure he's available on the day and happy to take on the role. Most men will be flattered, if a little scared – usually at the thought of making their speech. Chat

through what you expect and reassure him that you know he'll do an excellent job even if he doubts it himself, and buy him a copy of this book and one from our speechmaking range (see page 250). If he's going to be away on business during the run-up to the wedding, you may need to agree to delegate some of his jobs to someone else, perhaps your chief usher.

> ➤ Make sure you brief your best man on what is expected of him. You are the back-up if anything goes wrong!

If you have to choose between two good friends, you'll need to make a decision and stick to it. Speak to the other friend to make sure that he's not offended and perhaps find him another role for the wedding day if you feel that's appropriate and wouldn't upset him further.

Read through the Best Man chapter so you know what he's supposed to do and that you give him all the information and support he needs. If you know his organising skills aren't what they could be, you'll need to be behind him to make sure everything gets done. This is your sole responsibility, so make sure you don't blow it.

> ☺ Apart from the speech, the thing best men most dread is forgetting the rings or losing them. Buy a cheap spare ring yourself to rescue any disastrous situations, but don't tell anyone or he'll realise you don't trust him.

Why do I need ushers?

You don't – but it's a good way to involve brothers, friends or young relatives from both sides, and it's not a tough job. Read through their job description on pages 173–74 and decide whether you think you need them, then choose them in consultation with your best man. Basically, they are there to help organise transport (to get everyone from the church to the reception, for example), to hand out buttonholes and generally make themselves useful. The chief usher co-ordinates the others and acts as a stand-in for the best man. If the best man is going to leave the church with the wedding party to join the receiving line, the chief usher is the one who stays to organise the cars and make sure no one is stranded at the church.

Traditionally, of course, the ushers are male, but you don't have to stick to that, and there would be one to escort each bridesmaid (the chief bridesmaid being escorted by the best man). Nowadays, as far as numbers go, one usher for every 50 guests is about right, but be guided by your set-up and by common sense.

> ➤ Good sense, reliability, punctuality and friendliness are what you are looking for when choosing ushers. Try to avoid picking someone who has small children of his own to look after, unless they can be delegated to someone else for the day.

Make sure you familiarise yourself with the duties of the ushers. Then you can make sure that they have all the information they need to get on with the job. If there is anything they cannot do – for any reason – once again, it's down to you.

> ➤ Make sure the ushers have all the information they need to do their job. Read the Ushers chapter as well as this one.

What about a guard of honour?
If either you or your fianceé has a military or police background or is a member of a club or organisation, you could ask one of these organisations to form a guard of honour as you leave the ceremony.

The guest list
As we've said, the hosts at the reception are usually the bride's parents, so they'll be in charge of the guest list. You should have discussed numbers at the early meetings between the parents, and decided how many guests each family can invite. You then draw up a draft list with your mum and dad and talk that through with your fiancée's parents before making up the final list.

Of course, if you are paying for the whole thing, it's up to you. Just don't get too carried away.

> ➤ You won't receive an invitation to your own wedding – you're just expected to be there.

Who goes on the list?

Start with immediate family and closest friends, then work outwards. Don't be tempted to list every second cousin once removed. Think which people you really want to help you celebrate your wedding. Be realistic and consistent. Children can be tricky – if one of your cousins is allowed to bring their children, then you can assume that all the others will probably want to bring theirs as well, but if you meet regularly with one family and haven't seen the other since you were at nursery school, then you may be allowed to treat them differently.

> ➤ Try to be fair in the numbers you each agree to invite, but if your fiancée has a huge family and you have a small one, then don't expect the usual 50/50 split to apply.

What if there are too many people?

Cut down! If you've compiled the list in order of priority, then you have to start at the bottom. There are bound to be some people who can't come, so you can always put some names on a reserve list, then invite them later.

> ➤ Guests need to know whether they are invited to the whole thing, just to the reception, just to the party – or whatever – so clarity is essential. Make it clear, too, which children are included by actually naming them on the invitation.

Lots of people nowadays invite only the closest family and friends to the church and reception, then other friends and relatives are requested to join in the party in the evening. Alternatively, you could have a separate party for your less-close friends, although it does make them feel more part of the occasion if it all happens on one day.

> ✀£ You could offer to create the invitations on your PC to save printing costs. For an informal wedding, you could e-mail the invitations.

What about out-of-town guests?
If people are travelling a long distance, it's courteous to help them with finding overnight accommodation, although you don't have to pay for it. Ask for information from the hotel where the reception is being held, and find out about some local guest houses.

> ✂£ Ask friends to offer overnight accommodation to out-of-town guests.

What happens then?
Once you've drawn up the final list, the bride's parents will take over and send out the invitations. They will also receive and log the replies and send out any reserve invitations.

> ☺ If you have access to the internet, print off some maps showing the church and reception venues to send out with the invitations. Just go to **www.multimap.com**, tap in the postcode and it's all done for you.

The reception

The original purpose of a reception was to provide food for those who had travelled a long way to the ceremony and, although times have changed, things aren't all that different now. If your guests are going to be with you for most of the day, the least you can do is feed them! Anyway, it's a very sociable and hospitable thing to do and a great way to celebrate.

Much of the cost of a wedding relates to the reception. Of course, it doesn't have to cost thousands, but you do need to set a budget from the outset and stick to it (remember, we did that bit on page 22). The average cost for weddings in 2001, as we said earlier, was £8,000 but many couples spend a lot less (meaning that a few spend a lot more!), proving that with a little careful planning you can create a fabulous day whatever your budget.

It's usually the bride's parents who do most of the planning and booking, but it does no harm to show a constructive interest. If there are things that you particularly want to happen, then it's up to you to communicate your preferences to them.

What's a wedding breakfast?

It's just the old-fashioned term for the meal you have at the reception, based on the fact that weddings always used to be held in the morning, followed by the meal.

> ☺ Don't do the 'Shall we have cornflakes for the wedding breakfast?' gag more than once, please.

Is this going to be a formal affair?

Yes, no or maybe – it's up to you and your fiancée and the hosts. There is a huge range of options, as you can see from the ideas on the next page. Mix and match to suit whatever you feel you and your guests will most enjoy. Generally, the more formal the wedding, the more formal the reception – so a 'morning-suit' wedding gets a full sit-down meal with all the frills.

Venue	Guests	Meal	Drinks	Music	Invitations
Ultra-formal Grand hotel or ballroom	200+	Elaborate sit-down five-course dinner	Champagne throughout	Live orchestra or band	Engraved or printed
Formal Large hotel or marquee with caterers	150–200	Elegant sit-down dinner or sit-down buffet	Champagne throughout	Live band	Engraved or printed
Semi-formal Hotel	100–150	Sit-down dinner or sit-down buffet	Champagne for the toasts	Dance music/ disco	Printed
Informal Small hotel or club, hall with caterers or relatives and friends providing the food	Up to 100	Stand-up finger buffet	Champagne and/or wine	Disco	Printed or hand-written
Very informal Own home, relative or friend's home, or garden	As many as you can fit in	Sit-down fork buffet or stand-up finger buffet	Champagne and/or wine	CDs or taped music	Hand-written

What time?

This all knocks on from the time of the service, but you usually go straight from that to the reception venue. If there is to be an evening party, then the celebrations usually just keep going . . .

When choosing the food and setting the schedule, bear in mind how long your guests will have been without food before they arrive at the reception. If there is a long gap, suggest having some nibbles available to keep them going, especially if you are offering them alcohol as soon as they arrive.

If you have an early wedding and there's likely to be a gap between the end of the reception and the beginning of the evening party, try to sort out somewhere for the guests to relax for a bit, or something they can do. There's only so much time they can spend looking at wedding gifts, reading greetings cards, telemessages, telegrams and e-mails and drinking tea or alcohol! If they're left too long, the atmosphere may become sluggish.

☺ If there are children at the reception, make sure that they don't go without food of some kind for too long – hunger leads to tears and tantrums. A few bowls of crisps (not nuts) or fun-size bars is all it takes.

Who sits where at the reception?

The hosts will draw up a seating plan for all the guests. At a formal reception, there's a top table for the wedding party, with guests on the side tables. The traditional top table plan is:

Chief bridesmaid	Groom's father	Bride's mother	Groom	Bride	Bride's father	Groom's mother	Best man

This means that you sit in the middle on the right of your bride. Since it's an honour to sit at the top table, be careful not to cause any ruffled feathers by including a guest who's not also a member of the wedding party. However, if you have a really special guest – an aunt who has flown in from Australia specially, for example – you may want to make an exception.

If either set of parents is divorced, you'll need to be sensitive, the aim being to create the most friendly and relaxed atmosphere. If parents have remarried, their new partners should be asked to join the top table.

☺ Make sure you get a look at the table plan. The idea is that you try to mix people socially without leaving anyone completely separated from the people they know. Bear in mind any guests who are best kept on opposite sides of the room – this is not a time to raise old family disagreements or reunite old lovers.

What do I have to do about the reception?

Visit the reception venue with your fiancée and best man to find out where everything is. It's your best man's job to check whether there's going to be a toastmaster – if not, it's him – and a microphone for the speeches if you need it. He should also find out what the parking arrangements are like. You and the wedding party will arrive first at the reception and line up to receive your guests (yes, that's what a receiving line is), and the best man should have checked in advance to find the best spot for that. (Try not to have your guests queuing outside in the rain.)

Help your fiancée to choose and organise the music. If it's going to be a live band, you should listen to some of their sample tapes; hear them live, too, if you can. If it's a disco, try to get along to hear the sort of thing they play, or check their CD catalogue. If you are organising your own music, you could well get the job of putting some tapes together. Don't try to mess around with separate CDs – it's much better to have plenty of continuous tapes that you can just leave to do their own thing. Have some for background, some for dancing, think about the age range and remember that the corny party tunes ('Agadoo', anyone?) usually go down well after you've all had a few.

☺ Teenage cousins and weddings don't always mix; it's not really their kind of event. But you might trust one or two of them to be DJ for the reception – so long as you vet their choice of music in advance!

What about the drinks?

The drinks arrangements are pretty important so you should check those out. Is there to be a bar with staff? If so, are people paying for all their own drinks or is there going to be a free bar for some – or all – of the time? If drinks are going to be laid out on a side table, is it to be self-service or do you need bar staff? Are there any responsible youngsters who would like to help out?

> ✂£ Take a day trip to France to stock up on lots of inexpensive wine. Remember, however, unless you're having the reception in a private venue, you must check on reception corkage fees and add this to your cost calculations.

Don't ask the best man to be barman. Even for an informal reception, the wedding party members and important guests shouldn't be expected to tend the bar. You could ask a number of your friends to serve on a rota basis.

> ✂£ Good champagne is very expensive, but there are plenty of excellent sparkling wines and Spanish cavas that will go down just as well for the toasts.

What else is going to happen?

The full order of the day starts on page 235, but here's a rough idea.

You and your bride will arrive first at the reception, followed closely by your parents, the best man and the bridesmaids. You form a receiving line to welcome the guests. They will be offered a drink and everyone spends some time mingling and talking before the meal is served.

> ☺ Try to memorise some names and faces so you can recognise your wife's family when they arrive. Go through some family photos with your fiancée (other weddings are good) so she can point out some of her relatives.

At the end of the meal come the speeches (see pages 217–34) and then you cut the cake. Your bride holds the knife in her right hand, you place your right hand on top, then she places her left hand on top of that. Point the end of the knife at the centre of the bottom cake tier and slowly cut the cake. You and your bride share the first slice and the rest is sliced and circulated to the guests.

After that, there's usually a bit of a lull when the tables are cleared; that's a time for general mingling and conversation. Try to talk to as many of the guests as you can, and introduce your wife to those who haven't met her. When the music strikes up, you take your bride on to the floor for the first dance.

> ➤ It may be best to choose a slow dance for the first dance, but whatever you decide, make sure it's something you can dance to.

About halfway through, the parents will join you on the floor, then the best man and the chief bridesmaid. Then it's time for everyone to join in.

> ☺ Get your mum to teach you the basic steps of the waltz so you can dance with your grandma.

What's the arrangement at double weddings?

If you're marrying at the same time as another couple, the fiancées will need to plan very carefully. If the two brides are sisters, then the elder bride and her attendants take precedence; if the brides are not sisters, the elder groom's bride takes precedence.

Your best man will be one of two best men at a double wedding. He's responsible for your own particular party but when the duties overlap, such as for the full group photo and for the full receiving line, the senior groom's best man takes precedence.

☺ A fireworks display is a splendid way to round off an evening. Perhaps you could book and organise this as a gift to your bride (but be warned, it won't be cheap).

What about the toasts and the speeches?
This is probably what you are most worried about, so we've given them a whole chapter starting on page 217.

➢ Whatever else you serve, champagne is the traditional drink to toast the health of the bride and groom.

The honeymoon
Alone together at last! In the days when a groom captured his bride, the couple hid from her parents until the search was called off. After they were married, they'd hide for one full cycle of the moon while drinking honeyed wine, hence the expression 'honeymoon'.

Most couples leave for their honeymoon immediately after the wedding or on the following day, but that's up to you. It's certainly a good idea to have some relaxing time together immediately after the wedding, but if money is short, you may find it's better to spend just a weekend together away from it all, then save your honeymoon until your annual holiday when you've more cash to spare.

> ➤ Most couples have very high expectations of a honeymoon, and obviously you want it to be a holiday to remember. But don't forget that this is the culmination of a very demanding few months, and probably the most emotionally explosive day of your life, so give yourselves a little time to relax and wind down.

Where will we spend our first night?

If you want to stay at the reception and enjoy the party for as long as possible, you don't have to fly off on your honeymoon on the same day. Remember that it's going to be a long, exciting and emotionally charged day, so the thought of ending up spending the evening in an airport lounge may not be what you had in mind for your wedding night.

There are plenty of options, including going home, but it is nice to make it something a bit special. If there are suitable rooms available, it's a good idea to book into the reception hotel, or book somewhere close by so that you can officially 'leave' the reception – and just pop round the corner. Wherever you choose, make sure it's also convenient for any honeymoon travel plans you may have for the following day.

If you want to stay in the area, visit your local hotels and ask to see their bridal suites. Check what 'extras' are included in their honeymoon package – for example, some may offer a chauffeur-driven car to drive you to the airport in the morning.

Where should we go for our honeymoon?

It may sound obvious, but you need to book a honeymoon that appeals to both of you; if you follow your own interests while your wife trails along with little or no enthusiasm (or vice versa), that's hardly the best way to start married life! Think about what you both want to be doing on your honeymoon, read through the brochures and do the planning together, then you'll be sure to book something for you both.

Remember to think about your mode of transport. If one of you hates flying, for example, can you avoid it? Would a continental train journey be a romantic option?

Discuss what sort of accommodation you would prefer: hotel, pub, guesthouse, flat or apartment, cottage, caravan, tent, ship, boat, barge?

There are lots of different accommodation options: full board, half board, bed and breakfast, self-catering – which would you both prefer? If your fiancée tends to be the one to do the cooking, remember that she may well want time off on her honeymoon.

Choose a destination and style of holiday that suits you both. Here are a few ideas.

- A city such as Paris or Barcelona, where the attractions are not so dependent on the weather and you can indulge your appetite for culture and sight-seeing.
- The countryside for walking and relaxation, or sporting activities such as climbing.

- An adventure activity holiday.
- Sun, sea and sand where you can go for a lazy holiday and guarantee to come back with a tan.
- A cruise for a bit of on-board luxury.
- A luxury top hotel for total pampering.
- A hobby-based holiday learning to cook, painting or doing photography.
- A new experience, such as a health farm.

> ➤ **Never** revisit a destination where either of you has spent a holiday (or a honeymoon!) with a previous partner.

Timing may be an important consideration. Since honeymooners often go to more unusual destinations and not necessarily in the main holiday season, make sure you check the weather conditions at your destination before you book. The hurricane season in tropical countries is probably best avoided!

Can I keep the destination a secret?
If you want to surprise your fiancée, make sure she is happy with the idea of you choosing the destination. In any event, you'll probably have to give away some of the details, so that she can pack appropriately, and have an up-to-date passport and the right inoculations.

You don't have to tell anyone else where you are going if you don't want to.

What about the arrangements?

Choose a reputable travel agent who's a member of ABTA.
You'll need to organise:

- Flights and other travel arrangements.
- Hotel or accommodation reservations.
- Travel insurance – ensure that your insurance covers injury, sickness, lost property and travel delay.
- Passports.
- Travellers' cheques, foreign currency and credit cards.
- Inoculations, which should not be left to the last minute – you'll have enough to do in the run-up to the wedding without suffering the possible after-effects of an injection against cholera!

> ➤ Your fiancée's passport, tickets and travellers' cheques must all be in the same name. If she already has a passport, it's easiest to stick with her maiden name for the time being – even if she's changing her name – and take the wedding certificate with you. If she wants a new passport (and therefore everything else) in her married name, she'll need to apply three months before the ceremony and have it sent to the minister or registrar to keep until she is married.

What if we are on a tight budget?

I always think a holiday is a bit like betting: you should only pay out what you are happy to lose! You get plenty of wonderful things from a holiday, but not tangible things, and you want to be able to enjoy yourselves without constantly worrying about whether you can afford it, so choose sensibly.

Here's a whole list of ideas to help you plan a honeymoon on a budget.

- Time your wedding so that your honeymoon is in the off-season and therefore cheaper, or postpone the honeymoon until later to take advantage of cheap deals.
- Don't be shy about admitting your new status as some travel firms arrange special-offer honeymoon trips or bargain breaks complete with free champagne and four-poster beds, and hotels will often make a special effort for honeymooners.
- Some hotels offer a free night's accommodation for the bride and groom if they have a sizeable catered reception held in the hotel.
- Rent a holiday home and cater for yourselves. Ask relatives and friends who own a second home if they're prepared to rent it to you cheaply – or as a present.
- If you want sheer luxury but can't afford it, have just a weekend – it will work out the same price as a fortnight somewhere average.
- Choose a combined wedding/honeymoon package if this is cheaper.

- Travel on a weekday rather than a weekend.
- Book a last-minute holiday if you're not fussy about the destination but ensure that you've time to shop around just before the wedding. Get on the internet and see what's on offer.

What documents will we need?

Check off what you need from the list:

- Travel tickets.
- Insurance documents.
- Travellers' cheques.
- Spending money/foreign currency.
- Credit cards.
- Passports.
- Visas.
- Driving licences.
- Inoculations certificates.
- Marriage certificate if your wife's passport bears her maiden name.

Your best man should keep your documents safe on the wedding day. He'll hand them over to you when you leave the reception.

What should I pack?

Make sure that you don't forget anything. Use the Packing checklist on pages 111–12 as a starting point. Decide when you are going to pack, where you are going to park your cases, when you are going to pick them up, and work out in advance all the logistics of getting you and your belongings to where you need to be.

> ➤ The honeymoon arrangements are very much your responsibility – in combination with the best man – so you need to be in charge here.

What if we don't have a great time?

If something goes wrong while you are on holiday, tell the rep, hotel manager or whoever is in charge immediately – don't wait till you get home. They may well be able to sort it out and it's only fair to give them the chance to try. If you come back still feeling that you have a legitimate complaint, write clearly to the holiday company.

If you set your expectations beyond the stratosphere, don't be surprised if the honeymoon does not quite live up to all your hopes. The first few weeks of marriage are rarely problem-free. The two of you need time to learn to adjust to one another. Relax, take things as they come, and you'll soon find yourself looking back with affection on what will almost certainly be one of the most memorable holidays of your life.

Combined wedding and honeymoon packages

More and more couples are opting for an all-in-one package, so if the thought of saying your vows on a Caribbean beach sounds like your kind of thing, get hold of some brochures and investigate the possibilities.

One crucial point to remember is that legal requirements vary in each country and to come back legally wed, you'll need to fulfil both the requirements of this country and the country where the ceremony is to take place.

Another point to remember is that you have to think about the cost and travel implications for the people you want to be at the wedding. Most couples confine the guest list to the immediate family and friends for the wedding itself, which may mean disappointment for some who are not included. (Of course, for some people, getting away from the problem of who to invite is part of the attraction!)

To deal with this, you can throw a party for everyone else when you get home.

How do I organise this?

- Search bridal magazines for specialist holiday companies and ask ABTA for a list of specialist tour operators.
- Choose a package that suits your budget and unique requirements.
- Check whether any documentation has to be organised and paid for once you're there.

- Check on residency requirements.
- Check which name your bride will need on her passport.
- Obtain written confirmation including details of deposit and final payment terms.
- Obtain good insurance cover.
- Decide what you are both going to wear – a suit and tie may not be appropriate on a sun-kissed beach, but if your bride is going to choose an elegant silk number, she won't be too happy if you turn up in your Hawaiian shirt and shorts.
- Find out about a photographer – the hotel or your travel agent should be able to advise you here.
- Think carefully about your guest list. Make sure those you do invite are quite clear as to their financial commitments and give them plenty of information to help them make their own travel and accommodation bookings.
- Write to or contact close family and friends who are not going to be invited – but might otherwise expect to be on your list – and tell them that you are marrying abroad and only inviting a very small number. Consider having a party when you get home for those who did not come to the wedding.

What do I wear?

Wherever you get married, it is not really going to be up to you what you and the other male members of the wedding party wear: the bride will set the style for the whole thing, so follow her lead. You'd look pretty silly in morning dress if you are having a register office wedding and the bride is wearing a smart day-dress.

You probably won't actually see her dress until she turns up on the day, but you will be told whether you are expected to wear a morning suit or a lounge suit. You'll also be given a colour scheme for suits, ties, shirts, cummerbunds and so on, so you don't clash with bridesmaids and the flowers. Most brides like to colour-theme the whole thing, so she won't want you in a stunning purple shirt if everyone else is in pastels. It may sound a bit contrived, but it does make sense – the photos look much better. So make sure you know what she wants before you go out buying or hiring, and ask for a fabric sample so you can match the colours. Believe me, pink is never just pink.

☺ It's supposed to be very bad luck for the groom to see the bride in her wedding dress before the big day, so don't even try to find out – it's bound to cause a row.

What's the choice?

All the men in the wedding party men dress with the same degree of formality, so if it's morning dress for one, it's morning dress for you all. The rest of the male guests don't have to wear morning dress if you do, but they will be similarly smart. Sometimes all the male wedding party wear exactly matching outfits; sometimes the groom chooses to be slightly different in some way.

Top of the formality stakes is full morning dress. Generally, dark colours are worn for winter and afternoon weddings and lighter colours for summer and morning weddings. A traditional morning suit is a black or grey three-piece with tailcoat or a black tailcoat with pinstripe trousers, plus white shirt and grey tie, silk top hat and gloves. You are not actually required to wear the top hats, though morning dress is considered incorrect and incomplete unless you carry one. Hold it by the brim in your left hand. You should always remove it for the photos. Formal suits are now available in a wider range of colours; consult with the bride before you do anything rash.

> ➤ Deputise one of the younger ushers or a member of the family to keep track of all the top hats and gloves and make sure they are all retrieved after the photos.

For a less formal church wedding, you can choose a well-cut three- or two-piece lounge suit, preferably something you'll find useful after the wedding. If it is a second wedding for one of you, lounge suits are more usual.

For a civil ceremony, there tends to be more flexibility and less formality, but again you should be guided by the bride's dress. Registrars see everything from morning dress to jeans and T-shirts (not the most tasteful choice) but a smart lounge suit is the most appropriate option.

Co-ordinate and communicate

Once you have your instructions from the bride, talk to the other men about what is expected and what the colour scheme is, then make the arrangements for all of you to get your wedding outfits. Make sure you establish who is paying for what before you start. If you are hiring, it's probably down to you.

If you are hiring, try to get all the men together, go to the shop at the same time to be measured, and get the whole thing booked in one go. Pay the deposit, check the date for final payment and the collection and return arrangements. Shoes and any outstanding accessories should be sorted out by each individual, so make sure they all know that.

Don't leave hiring to the last minute, especially for a summer wedding, or you could find that everyone else is getting married on the same day and you can't get what you want. There are plenty of places in the high street where you can hire suits, and there's more information on the internet if you want to do the groundwork from your desk.

> ✂£ Few people have their own formal wear or need to wear it regularly, so it's more sensible to hire it than buy it.

If the men in the wedding party are buying their own suits, make sure you are clear about colour and style so that you all co-ordinate well. You also don't want anyone to outshine you. For instance, if your best man wears navy when everyone else is in grey, he will be the one who stands out rather than you! It's a good idea to take your best man along with you when you go suit-shopping.

> ✂£ If you have plenty of time, go to the sales to buy your suit. You can often get good bargains, so you can have a much better-quality suit than you might otherwise be able to afford.

Choose your shoes, shirt and tie at the same time and don't forget small details like socks.

Formal menswear

Here's an idea of the formality options. You should choose black lace-up shoes and black socks. Otherwise, shoes and socks are generally black or to match the suit.

Formal traditional style (day): Black or grey tailcoat; black, grey or pinstripe trousers with cummerbund or plain or patterned, grey, double- or single-breasted waistcoat; white shirt with double cuffs and cufflinks; grey silk cravat; black or grey silk top hat; yellow chamois gloves for black coat, grey gloves for grey coat.

Formal modern style (day): Jacket and trousers as above; patterned waistcoat; white shirt with turn-down collar; grey or navy silk tie; top hat and gloves as above.

Formal traditional style (evening): Tailcoat; pinstripe trousers; waistcoat to match tie; white shirt with double cuffs and cufflinks; bow tie; black top hat, gloves.

Formal modern style (evening): Black dinner jacket; black trousers; cummerbund or waistcoat optional; white shirt with wing collar; bow tie.

Semi-formal (day): Black or grey lounge suit; grey waistcoat; white shirt with soft collar, double cuffs and cufflinks; plain pale blue or grey tie.

Semi-formal (evening): Dinner jacket with silk lapels; black trousers with optional cummerbund; dress shirt; bow tie.

Informal (day or evening): Lounge suit; white or coloured shirt to match the suit; tie to match.

Members of the armed forces may wear uniform in conjunction with any of the above. Another popular option for those with Scottish connections is Highland dress.

The flowers

The tradition of the bride carrying flowers has its roots in ancient times when it was believed that strong-smelling herbs and spices would ward off evil spirits, bad luck and ill health. But why do **you** need to know about the flowers, you may ask? Well, one good reason is that you are paying for some of them.

The groom usually pays for the bride's and bridesmaids' bouquets, any flowers for their headdresses, flowers for the buttonholes of the principal men, and corsages for the two mothers. These will probably be ordered along with the flowers for the church and reception, for which the bride's family pay. The bride may also want flowers in the bridal cars.

The bride will know what colours and what type of bouquets she wants, and the style of the buttonholes and corsages. She may or may not want you to visit the florist and make the choices with her. You should certainly know about the collection and payment arrangements.

> ☺ For a surprise romantic touch, ask the florist to strew the marquee floor with fresh herbs, such as rosemary for remembrance and myrtle for love, so that they release their fragrance when trodden. (But keep them away from the dance floor.)

What about buttonholes, corsages and sprays?

The male members of the wedding party usually wear a flower in their left buttonhole, while the two mothers each have a corsage – this is a few flowers in a mini-bunch. A single red or white carnation is the favourite buttonhole, but the bride may prefer a rose, orchid or camellia. The mothers' corsages will be co-ordinated with the colour their outfits.

> ☺ It's best if the best man or one of the ushers picks up the flowers from the bride's house, just in case you see her – very unlucky!

If you have not made the arrangements yourself, you or the best man must find out when and where the flowers are being delivered (usually to the bride's home), so that someone can collect them and take them to the church in good time. Check whether anything else needs to be collected or delivered at the same time, and allow plenty of time.

☺ Start a new trend by throwing your buttonhole to the assembled pageboys and ushers after the bride has tossed her bouquet towards the bridesmaids. You never know, it may catch on!

The transport

You have to book and pay for the transport for:
- You and your best man to the church.
- You and your bride to the reception.
- You and your bride from the reception to the first-night venue.

The best man does the on-the-day organising, so bring him in on the early stages, and make sure you are both agreed on what each of you is doing.

How do I go about it?

Magazines, Yellow Pages, local papers, the internet – it's easy to find a handful of places to ring for quotes on car hire before you make your comparisons and fix the booking. The bride may do this herself, or leave it to you. Make sure you pay the deposit on time, and note down the final payment date so you don't miss it and lose the transport.

There are several things you should think about when making your choice.

- What does the bride want?
- How much can you afford?
- Who's going to drive? It's not a good idea to drive yourself. Apart from anything else, it means you have to park it.
- What if it rains? If it's an open-topped car, make sure it has a hood.
- What about the bride's dress? Don't go for a sleek sports car if she has a huge dress.

✄£ Use your own car or borrow from a friend rather than hiring if you wish, but do get someone to drive for you.

What are the choices? Pretty much endless, but here are some ideas.

- Rolls Royce.
- Veteran car.
- Stretch limousine.
- Pony and trap.
- Coach and four.
- Sedan chair.
- Taxi – normal or white London taxi.
- Bus.
- The latest and flashest car you can get.
- Helicopter (I said the choices were endless).

✂£ If you are organising your own transport, either you or the best man will need to buy the ribbons. There's no need to buy silk ribbons. You can buy florist's ribbon by the roll (rather than by the metre) – it is much cheaper and will look just as good.

The presents

You and your fiancée generally buy presents for all the wedding party to thank them for their support and hard work in all the planning and on the day. There are some gifts that you and your fiancée will choose together and others that you have to sort out on your own, so find out what is down to you and make sure you find something appropriate in good time.

Technically, you buy each of the bridesmaids a gift and the bride buys one for each of the pageboys, although it's usually a joint thing. (Originally, gifts for the bridesmaids were a bribe from the groom to persuade the bride's friends to lure her to a place where the groom could meet her.) You buy a gift for the best man. The ushers don't traditionally receive gifts, but many couples like to give them a small token of their appreciation.

Try to make your choices personal ones. Many people like to keep their gift as a memento of the occasion, or you might like to personalise gifts with your names and the wedding date.

What should we buy ?

Bridesmaids: Jewellery is the hot favourite and there's so much choice of style and budget you can't go far wrong. For younger girls, you could think about soft toys, a jewellery box, or a Barbie doll dressed in the same bridesmaid's dress.

☺ If you decide to buy earrings for the bridesmaids, make sure your fiancée checks whether they have had their ears pierced. Imagine how disappointed they'll be if you give them earrings for pierced ears and they can't wear them.

Pageboys: Computer game, CDs, videos, a football, tickets to a match.

☺ Especially if you have failed in your task of avoiding velvet knee breeches and frills, make sure you buy the pageboys something they will enjoy *now*. After all, would you like a pair of personalised cufflinks as a reward for having your street cred ruined for months?

Best man: Hip flask, tankard, bottle of malt whisky, bottle of fine wine, watch, camera, crystal decanter, paperweight, clock, fountain pen, business card holder, tickets to an event.

Ushers: Tankard, bottle of fine wine, bottle of malt whisky, wallet, leather gloves.

☺ Cufflinks and tie-pins always seem to appear on these lists. They may be convenient things to give, but I'm not convinced they are such fun to receive. Think about whether your friends would ever take them out of the box.

Parents: Commemorative dishes, engraved jewellery, glassware, crystal decanters, engraved paperweights, theatre or concert tickets. Simplest and perhaps best of all, wedding photos in ornamental frames.

> ☺ Arrange for a bunch of flowers or a bottle of champagne to be delivered to your parents and your fiancée's parents the day after the wedding with a thank you note.

When do we give the gifts?

It's best to avoid giving the gifts on the wedding day itself. There will be too many things to think about, and anyway it makes it much more personal to choose a time when everything is less hectic. The rehearsal get-together is usually the best moment.

> ☺ If you give out your gifts when other people are present, make sure there is no one there who is not receiving something.

What about gifts for the guests?

This is really up to the hosts. Sometimes they put balloons, streamers, party poppers or flings (something I've just discovered that appears to be like a very up-market streamer) on the reception tables for the guests.

> ✂£ This is serious break-the-budget country. Enter at your peril.

Some hosts buy a present for each guest. Ideas include teddy bears, bags or decorative boxes of sweets, chocolate coins, bottles of bubbles, personalised champagne flutes. However, unless you've just won the lottery or you don't know the meaning of the word 'budget', I'd advise you to steer clear.

> ☺ You might like to buy some disposable cameras for your reception tables. These give guests something to do and you might get some good informal behind-the-scenes shots to supplement your wedding album.

What about a gift for the bride?

The wedding ring is your gift to the bride, although many men also buy a personal item of jewellery as well. It's not actually a legal requirement to give a ring, but it is traditional and it's a lovely symbol of enduring love. Most brides have now adopted the continental idea of buying a wedding ring for the groom. Most people buy a new ring, but you could also buy an antique or second-hand ring, or pass on a family heirloom. If you are seriously flush, you could commission a jeweller to design you a one-off ring. The choice ranges from a plain band of gold to the fairly ornate. Shop around because prices vary considerably.

Here are some things to think about when you are making your choice.

Comfort: You'll be wearing your ring most of the time so make sure it is comfortable.

Compatibility: Your fiancée will probably wear her ring with her engagement ring so make sure they sit together well.

Durability: The most popular metal is 18-carat gold because it stands up to many years' wear. (22- and 24-carat gold are softer.)

Quality: Buy from a reputable shop for the best quality goods.

Receipt: Always get a receipt. This should include the cost, carat weight, gem description and quality, if appropriate, plus policy regarding exchange, refund, repair or replacement.

Guarantee: Make sure you get a written guarantee and keep it in a safe place.

Valuation: If you are buying second-hand, have the item valued by a qualified appraiser and get a valuation certificate.

Insurance: Once you have bought the ring, make sure it is covered by your house contents insurance.

Time: Allow enough time to have the rings engraved, if you wish.

About wedding rings

There are various grades of gold you can buy, and each has different qualities.

Metal	Colour	% purity	Carat	Durability	Cost and availability
Platinum	White			Very durable	Most expensive
Gold	Very strong natural yellow	100	24	Very soft and heavy	Very expensive and more difficult to find
	Strong yellow	91.6	22	Soft and fairy heavy	Expensive and less common than 18 carat
	Medium yellow	75	18	Hard	Practical and the most readily available
	Light yellow	37.5	9	Hardest	Least expensive
	White		18	Hard	More expensive than ordinary gold as it is less commonly available
	White		9	Harder	Not widely available
	Red				Not widely available

The hallmark on a ring will tell you the details of where and when it was made. There are five symbols on the hallmark.

Manufacturer's initials	A crown	Carat number	Assay office (for Britain)	Alphabetically coded date stamp
		916=22 750=18 585=14 375= 9	Leopard=London Anchor=Birmingham Rose=Sheffield Castle=Edinburgh	The style changes every 26 years but it is now no longer a requirement to symbolise the date B = 1975 G = 1980 L = 1985 Q = 1990 V = 1995 Z = 1999 a = 2000

What about gifts for me – and us?

The bride will probably buy you a ring, and perhaps also a personal gift of jewellery or something similar, but that's it for you, I'm afraid.

Apart, of course, from the gifts that the guests give to you as a couple. Your fiancée will probably compile the wedding gift list, which not only means that you receive gifts you really want and need, but also helps you if you are building up sets of things (a dinner service, for example). It also helps to avoid overlaps, and reassures the guests that they are buying something that you will really like. If you are setting up a new home together, the list will primarily include household items, although if you already have most of the practical items you need, or if you are combining two households, you can afford to be a bit more adventurous.

You can help to compile the list by thinking of items that your fiancée may not have thought of. She may have her own DIY tool kit and be a far better gardener than you, but then again she may see that as your province. Concentrate on the areas you know about. If you are the cook in the household, you should be choosing the saucepans. At the risk of gender stereotyping (but you wouldn't want 'sewing machine' on your list, would you?), here are some areas you might think about: DIY, garden tools or furniture, home security, barbecue equipment, luggage, TV, video, stereo, CDs.

You can include some personal items on the list, but guests are really giving things to you as a couple rather than individuals, so if you need a new casual jacket, tough luck. On the other hand, you might like to include pictures, photo frames, a subscription to a homes magazine or gift vouchers.

☺ It's a nice idea to ask someone to buy you a specific gift as a compliment to their particular skills. If your uncle is an expert carpenter, he would be flattered to be asked to choose you a set of chisels, for example.

Can we ask for money?

It used to be considered bad form to ask for money, and equally bad form for anyone other than close family to give money, but that's not the case any more. Most people will be happy to give you a gift of money, especially if you are saving towards a major purchase, or you want to put the money to a deposit on a house, for example.

Do bear in mind, however, that some older guests may be uncomfortable about giving money, so think of something to ask them to buy instead. Also, some people may not be able to spend a lot of money on a present. Don't embarrass people by putting them in a situation they might find difficult.

> ➤ Remember that the value of a present is not in how much it cost but in the thought and effort that went into buying or making it.

In any event, make sure you put all the money in a separate and safe place so that it doesn't get absorbed in your day-to-day expenses. That would be a waste of an opportunity for you and probably upset quite a few people as well. Decide how you are going to use the money and be firm about it.

Thank you letters

Always acknowledge gifts with a letter of thanks. It doesn't have to be long or formal, but it is important that it is personal.

A printed thank you note (you know the sort of thing – no room for a name and a dotted line to fill in the gift) is the height of rudeness. The bride may do many of the notes, but you should write to your friends and family, so buy a pack of notelets, dust off your quill and get writing. If you have received a gift of money, don't mention the amount in your letter, but do tell the person how you plan to spend it.

> ☺ Younger guests may be quite happy with an e-mail thank you, but older guests might find it a bit off-hand. A card or letter is more acceptable.

Party! Party! Party!

One of the great things about being the most important man is that you get to go to all the parties – with the notable exception of the hen night.

How many parties do I get to enjoy?

The family get-together: This is the first time your parents and your future bride's parents meet to begin to get to know each other and to talk about the wedding (see page 21). It provides an opportunity to discuss the wedding style and arrangements, who's going to do what, and who's going to pay.

The engagement party: Usually thrown by the bride's parents, this is when her father announces the engagement (see page 22). Even if everyone knows already, he is likely to say a few words of congratulation, so be prepared to say a few words of thanks to your hosts and something romantic about your new fiancée, and to propose a toast to both sets of parents.

> ☺ Help with the clearing up. Little, thoughtful gestures like that will get you in everyone's good books.

Guests aren't expected to bring gifts, but they probably will. Don't lose track of who gave you what, so you can send thank you letters.

> ☺ Offer to write the thank you letters, or at least to your friends and family. After all, why should the girl do it all?

A party for friends: If you can't invite everyone to the wedding, you and your fiancée may want to throw an evening party for friends and colleagues you haven't included on the wedding list.

The rehearsal get-together: For a big wedding, there's likely to be a rehearsal, and you and your fiancée may like to organise a get-together for the wedding party after the rehearsal to thank them for all their hard work beforehand and on the day. It could be a small party at home, a dinner party, or a meal at a local restaurant. You usually invite both sets of parents, the best man, the bridesmaids and ushers. It's an ideal time to thank them for their support and to give them any gifts you have bought for them.

Some grooms also use this as an opportunity to make sure their best man has made all the arrangements for the big day, and to pass on any information like the seating arrangements for the reception. However, it's sometimes better not to mix business and pleasure (especially since he may have forgotten everything by the time he sobers up next day), so you may want to do that another time.

✄£ If you're strapped for cash, forget this get-together but don't forget to make the time to thank everyone individually for their support and any gifts.

The stag night: This deserves its own section, so see page 89.

An after-the-wedding party: Once all the excitement has died down and you are back from your honeymoon, you can invite both sets of parents, the best man, bridesmaids and ushers to your new home for a meal to say thank you. You may also want to entertain anyone who could not come to the wedding but gave you a gift.

The stag night

You don't need reminding that this is when you and your mates celebrate the end of your bachelor freedom. Fortunately, the habit of holding the stag night on the eve of the wedding has all but died out. That was a seriously bad idea! You know they are going to get you slaughtered and you know what you are like with a hangover – enough said. Hold it the weekend before the wedding, stock up on orange juice, still mineral water and seltzer, and cancel everything else for 48 hours afterwards.

➤ Write your name and address and the number of a reliable local taxi firm on your forearm before you go, just in case.

The job of organising the event falls to your best man – he's also supposed to get you and the other guests home safely afterwards – so chat to him about what you would like, and who to invite. Include your dad and brothers as well as your fiancée's father and brothers, the ushers and your closest friends. Set the date, time and format for the evening, and let the best man make the invitations. If there's a large group of you, he may need to book in advance, especially for a meal.

☺ You may like to know that the fathers are supposed to show good form by leaving early.

The most popular stag nights involve a meal, several pubs and perhaps a nightclub. If all the guests live in the same town, that makes the ideal location easy. But if this is not the case, you could perhaps meet at a central location and all organise overnight accommodation, or just organise accommodation for those travelling any distance.

Whatever you decide to do, **don't drive**. The best man should either book taxis, or have the numbers of a couple of local firms so you can call taxis when you are ready to throw in the towel (or throw up in a bucket).

☺ Once it's all over, text or phone your fiancée to say you're home safely (or ask the best man to do so) so she doesn't spend all night worrying. Little thoughtful gestures like this will be very well received. Under no circumstances should you turn up outside her window with all your drunken mates to serenade her.

Traditionally the groom paid for the whole evening (but then traditionally it was a black tie affair at a gentlemen's club) but these days your friends will expect to pay at least some of the expense. Tell your best man how much you will pay for so he can make sure everyone knows when to chip in. You may decide you will pay for the meal, then have a kitty for the drinks, in which case the best man should be in charge of that. Alternatively, your friends may decide to follow more recent practice where they pay a set price that also covers **your** expenses for the evening.

> ✄£ If you are seriously short of funds, what about a couple of videos, a crate of beer and a take-away?

A stag weekend or event

Today's stag dos are all about originality and style, so if you fancy something different, how about a complete stag weekend, or going to an event with your mates? Take a look on the internet, at the travel agent's or in the wedding magazines – your fiancée will probably have plenty – and you'll see specially organised adventure holidays, golfing breaks or city weekends, which range from thrilling to lazy, from cultural to luxurious. For an unforgettable pre-wedding bash, start planning early and be creative.

> ☺ Don't embarrass your friends by choosing something they'll find it hard to afford, and do be up-front about the cost. You may be able to offer options: a small group going somewhere for the weekend, with others joining you for the main evening's entertainment.

Here are some ideas to get you thinking.

- Surfing, water-skiing or white-water rafting.
- Skiing or snow boarding – the real thing or on a dry slope.
- Fly-fishing or sea angling.
- Parascending or parachuting.
- An adventure activity holiday.
- Going to a horse- or dog-racing meeting.
- A round of golf or a golfing weekend – somewhere where there's a good nineteenth hole.
- Going to a major sporting event such as a Formula 1 meeting or an international rugby or football match.
- A day at a theme park (to get in touch with your inner child!).
- Driving Ferraris, 4x4s or off-roaders.
- A music concert – whatever you fancy, rock, jazz or classical.
- A city break to Paris, Barcelona or a British city such as Edinburgh or Bath.
- A tour of Scottish whisky distilleries or French vineyards.
- A meal at a top restaurant.

Another modern option is to combine the stag and hen parties and go out for a meal or to a nightclub.

Panic, stress and cold feet

So you are going to remain cool, calm and collected throughout the whole organising and planning phase. You are not going to worry about going over-budget or finding a ring that she actually likes. You are definitely not going to break out in a cold sweat when you try on your made-to-measure suit a week before the big day (because you've left it to the last minute) and it appears to have been made to measure someone else. Good for you – you really are one in a million! For more normal males, here's a quick run-down on how to cope with nerves.

Compromise and prioritise

This is the run-up to one of the most important days in your life – and your fiancée's. There will be stresses, strains and probably arguments. The important thing is to try to retain your sense of proportion. When things get tough, hang on to the thought that you've decided to commit yourselves to each other, you're in love and want to celebrate the wedding day in the most wonderful and memorable way. It's the commitment and the joy that matter, not the colour of the car or the fact that the napkins match the balloons or whether the flowers turn up on time.

Since there are not just two people but two whole families involved, you'll both have to learn to compromise. Be prepared to give way on some things, and your fiancée will do the same on others. There may also be compromises on budget. Don't be fooled by advertisers into thinking that the more you spend, the better the day will be; it can be wonderful whatever you spend – and you can make it so. Make your decisions together on what your priorities are, then try to stick to them; make savings elsewhere as necessary. If inviting everyone you know is the most important thing, go for an informal buffet reception. If you want to drink vintage champagne all day, served by sophisticated waiters in dinner jackets, keep your guest list to a minimum.

> ☺ Every bride has her own ideas on what is really important to her. Her choices may not stand up to logical examination, but they are no less important for that, so do at least give them consideration. If something seems really to matter to her, try to make it happen.

Coping with stress

The best trick of all is spotting the stress building up and releasing it before it blows. You know that moment when the sauce in the pan is about to boil, and you whip it off just in time before it makes a horrible mess on the cooker? This is just the same. If you are getting angry about something or you can see she is getting worked up, don't just sit around and hope it will blow over. The odds are that it'll blow up.

Here are a few stress-busting ideas. Commit them to memory – you may find them useful in your married life, too.

Communicate: Try to get her to talk about what is worrying her, and tell her what is bothering you. That may be enough to release the pressure, and you may find a compromise, or see a simple solution that the other person has missed.

Take time out: A weekend away – even a day or an evening – when wedding talk is banned will work wonders.

Laugh: If you can see the funny side of things, you'll find it much harder to lose your sense of proportion.

Give in (occasionally): Find something that doesn't make that much difference to you but is important to her, and back down.

Be understanding: Your fiancée may well get stressed out at things that don't seem to matter to you at all. Try to understand, but if you can't, bluff it.

Be generous: Buy her a bunch of flowers, a box of chocolates or something she likes.

Be family-friendly: Offer to take her father down the pub or to a match. Offer to take her parents out for a meal.

Be romantic: Buy her a cuddly toy, or send a romantic card or e-mail (you may think it's cheesy, but she'll appreciate it).

Be sexy: Let her know that you don't just want her for her marquee and canapés. You might not have forgotten, but she could have.

Be spontaneous: Turn up on a Saturday morning with two tickets to Paris (or a rock concert or a caravan in Bournemouth – whatever) and a toothbrush.

Be comfortable: Get a video (**not** *Rambo*), a bottle of wine and a take-away and slob out together in front of the TV for the evening.

Be assertive: Ring up that bolshie florist for her and find out why she can't deliver the corsages before breakfast.

Be individual: Maintain your own interests and allow your fiancée to maintain hers. You'll both remain far more interesting to each other if you don't live in each other's pockets all the time.

☺ Don't forget it's simple and cheap to send a text message, but the timing is crucial. You don't have to be any more imaginative than 'I love you' if you send it when she least expects it.

Last-minute nerves

Getting cold feet? Last-minute nerves? You and every other prospective groom (and bride, and bride's mother ...). Sometimes it's hard to see why you are putting yourselves through such a mammoth task of organisation and expense when all you want is to be together.

Hold that last bit. You **will** be together, having had the most wonderful day that you will always remember. It will be a great thing to relive when you have one of those **very** long weeks, or after you've had a blazing row and you are both sitting sulking in separate rooms. All the skills you'll have learned through this testing time will be very useful in your married life. Look at the list on the last two pages – use it!

Think about everyone else as well

The other thing to remember is that although you and your fiancée are centre stage, this is really important to your families too, especially both your mums. They may not share your perspective on everything, they may drive you barmy from time to time, but they'll be busting a gut to do their best for you.

☺ By the time you discover the truth of the corny old adage that there's nothing quite like the love of a parent for their child, you may have missed plenty of opportunities to let yours know you appreciate them and return their love for you.

Especially if you are living at home, your parents have to come to terms with the fact that their relationship with their son will never be the same again – and that also means admitting that they are getting older. They may brazen it out, but few people face that with true equanimity. Think about how much you take for granted: a clean house, a cheap landlord, clean washing, expert cooking, a free chauffeur, all the shopping done. The more you've let your mum do for you, the bigger the hole in her daily routine will be when you go. If you haven't yet figured out how to work the washing machine, now's the time to learn. It's no excuse to say your dad can't use it either, or that your mum does it quicker. In fact, it just emphasises that you should have taken more responsibility years ago.

Being able to put your sports kit in the washing machine all on your own or hang clothes on the line without being prompted will prove immensely useful when you are trying to keep in your new wife's good books – for whatever reason. But it will also free up more of your parents' time to get used to being themselves again, rather than your parents, or to pick up on old hobbies. Encourage them to go dancing, do the garden, sign up for an evening class, dust off the paint brushes – whatever takes their fancy. The greatest compliment you can pay them for all their hard work is that you turned out a thoughtful young man, and that sets a secure foundation for a realistic and ongoing friendly relationship with them.

The groom's diary

Run through this with your fiancée and personalise it to suit your own arrangements, then make sure you use it to tick off the jobs you have done, and remind you about the ones you haven't. The timing will vary for everyone, but this gives you a good rule of thumb. Many of the jobs will be done with your fiancée.

When you get engaged
- ❏ Tell your fiancée's parents and then your parents.
- ❏ Tell everyone else.
- ❏ Help with the arrangements for the engagement party.
- ❏ Arrange a meeting with the parents to set the style, the budget and the payment arrangements.

Six months before
- ❏ Check the availability of reception and ceremony venues so you can set the date.
- ❏ Make a draft guest list with your parents, then liaise with your fiancée's parents to finalise the list.
- ❏ Make your suggestions for the wedding gift list.
- ❏ Choose and book the ceremony venue.
- ❏ Choose and book the reception venue.
- ❏ Choose and book the musical entertainment.
- ❏ Meet the minister to organise the banns or organise the registrar's certificate.

❏ Choose and brief your best man and ushers.
❏ Plan and book the honeymoon.
❏ Book time off work.
❏ Start home-hunting.

Four months before

❏ Go through the six-month checklist and make sure everything has been done.
❏ If you are hiring, book the suits for the principal men.
❏ If you're buying, shop now for your own suit and accessories.
❏ Make sure all the men have bought their outfits. Don't forget accessories.
❏ Arrange the transport.
❏ Check your passports and any special visas and travel documents you need for the honeymoon.
❏ Check whether you need any inoculations and get them organised.
❏ Start thinking about furnishing your new home.

Three months before

❏ Make sure you know who's who in the wedding party.
❏ Make sure you have a suitable going-away outfit and do all your shopping for the honeymoon.

Two months before

❑ Choose and buy the wedding rings.
❑ Buy and wrap your gift for the bride.
❑ Buy and wrap your gifts for the best man and ushers.
❑ Buy the ribbons for the wedding cars.
❑ Go through the ceremony arrangements and obtain your marriage licence or schedule.
❑ Find out who will be making speeches, and the order of the speeches.
❑ Write your speech.
❑ Make sure your best man has all the information he needs and that he has written his speech.
❑ Arrange the stag night.

One month before

❑ Make sure you know about the rehearsal arrangements.
❑ Attend church for the reading of the banns.
❑ Finalise and pay for the transport.
❑ Pay for the buttonholes, flowers for the bride and her female attendants and corsages for the bride's mum and yours.
❑ Check the seating plan. Give a copy to the best man and the ushers.
❑ Finalise and pay for the honeymoon.
❑ Order any currency or travellers' cheques, if necessary.
❑ Prepare to move into your new home.

The week before

- ❑ Attend the rehearsal.
- ❑ Attend church for the final reading of the banns.
- ❑ Collect the banns certificate or wedding certificate.
- ❑ Finalise and pay for the transport.
- ❑ Make sure the best man knows when and where to collect the order of services sheets and the buttonholes.
- ❑ Get your outfit ready, or collect it if hired, polish your shoes and remove any price tags.
- ❑ Have a hair cut.
- ❑ Recover from the stag night.
- ❑ Pack for the honeymoon.
- ❑ Check all your honeymoon documents, including your credit card, and collect your currency and travellers' cheques.
- ❑ Ask a neighbour, friend or your best man to keep an eye on your home and car while you're away.
- ❑ Pay any bills that may fall due while you're honeymooning.
- ❑ Arrange for someone to return any hired items after the wedding.
- ❑ Arrange for the honeymoon luggage and going-away clothes to be taken to the reception venue.

The day before

- ❑ Check all the lists to make sure you've done everything.
- ❑ Double-check your outfit.
- ❑ Check petrol levels in any borrowed cars.

On the day

This is hardly the day to be ticking boxes, but there are a few things you should do before leaving the house.

❑ Check that your luggage, going-away outfit, going-away car and all your documents are at the reception venue.

❑ Give the church fees, documentation and ring(s) to your best man, with some spare cash for incidentals.

❑ Put your notes for your speech in your pocket.

Since you are involved in pretty much everything, there's a full run-through of the day's events starting on page 235. Customise it, highlight it, personalise it – whatever helps. You may want to copy it for the best man and highlight the bits that are important to him, although there's a briefer version for each of the principal men in their own chapters.

After the honeymoon

❑ Write thank you letters to all the wedding party, and finish any outstanding thank you letters for gifts.

❑ Check that all hired items have been returned.

❑ Entertain both sets of parents, then the best man and chief bridesmaid and bridesmaids in your new home during the three months following the wedding.

❑ Write to anyone who needs to know about your married status. This includes insurance companies for the beneficiary on policies, etc.

❏ Send out personal change-of-address cards, if necessary.
❏ Change your doctor and dentist if you've moved a considerable distance.
❏ Make new wills, as marriage automatically renders previous wills invalid.

The groom's data

Use the following pages to jot down all the information you need to keep handy. The 'who's who' lists will help you to remember everyone's names.

The engagement party

Make a note of the people on your side of the family you would like invited to the party, then copy it to the hosts, or talk to them about it. Remember that your fiancée's parents are likely to be paying for the party. Since they are the hosts, they will keep a record of who is able to come, or you can tick them off on your list.

Name	Address	Telephone	E-mail

The wedding party

Role	Name	Address	Telephone	Mobile	E-mail
Bride's mother					
Bride's father					
Groom's mother					
Groom's father					
Best man					
Chief usher					
Usher					
Usher					
Chief bridesmaid					
Bridesmaid					
Bridesmaid					
Flower girl					
Pageboy					
Pageboy					
Witnesses					
Special guests					

Guest list for groom's family and friends

Use this to create a draft list with your parents, then liaise with your fiancée's parents, who will draw up the final list, send out the invitations and receive the replies.

Name	Address	Telephone	Special needs	Definite	Possible

Total number of definites:
Total number of possibles:

Ceremony details

It's likely that the bride will take the lead in this discussion, but you'll be paying for a lot of it and be responsible for the paperwork, so you need to be up to speed on what is going on. Much of this applies to a church ceremony rather than a civil wedding. Jot down the dates of meetings and rehearsals in your diary.

If your fiancée is concentrating on listening to the minister, it can be useful if you can jot down details. She'll appreciate your attention to detail.

Location:

Church or register office	
Minister or registrar	
Address	
Telephone	
Date of ceremony	
Time of ceremony	
Residency requirements	
Groom's church or register office	
Minister or registrar	
Address	
Telephone	

First interview:

Interview date		
Interview time		
Take with you	Birth certificate	
	Death certificate (if widowed)	
	Decree absolute (if divorced)	
	Pen and paper	
Things to discuss	Type of service: 1662 1928	
	1980/2000	
	Maximum size of congregation	
	Order of service	
	Blessing	
	Readings	
	Hymns	
	Psalm	
	Music	
	(processional/recessional)	
	Soloist	
	Cost of organist	
	Cost of choir	
	Soloist	
	Cost of bell-ringers	
	Are flowers allowed?	
	Are photographs allowed?	
	Is a video allowed?	
	Is confetti allowed?	

The groom

Pre-wedding meetings:

Date		Time	
Date		Time	
Date		Time	
Date		Time	
Date		Time	
Rehearsal date		Rehearsal time	

Reading the banns:

Location	Date	Time of service
Bride's church	1	
	2	
	3	
Groom's church	1	
	2	
	3	

Honeymoon packing:

Type	Item	Packed
Documents	Passports	
	Visas	
	Marriage certificate	
	Travellers' cheques	
	Credit cards	
	Foreign currency	
	Insurance documents	
	Inoculations certificate	
	Driving licence	
	Travel tickets	
	Car keys	
	Essential telephone numbers	
Toiletries	Toilet bag	
	Shaving gear	
	Plug adapter	
	Contraception	
	Sunscreen	
	Towels	

Honeymoon packing (cont):

Type	Item	Packed
Clothes	Coats/jackets	
	Shirts	
	Trousers	
	Suit/smart clothes	
	Casual clothes	
	Underwear	
	Shoes	
	Nightwear(!)	
Miscellaneous	Camera	
	Films	
	Batteries	
	Camcorder/video	
	Books	
	Personal CD or cassette	
	Sports equipment	

Menswear

You need to sort out your own outfit, of course, but you'll probably be the point of liaison between all the men in the wedding party to let them know what they should be wearing and to make sure they have everything. Keep a note of all the details you need, and tick off on the list when you have confirmed that your support team have everything they need for the day.

Menswear supplier	
Address	
Telephone	
E-mail	
Fitting date	
Collection date	
Return date	
Person to return	
Cleaning arrangements	
Style/colour of jacket, trousers and waistcoat	
Style/colour of shirt	
Style/colour of tie	
Costs	
Deposit amount and payment date	
Balance amount and payment date	

The groom

Item	Groom	Best man	Bride's father	Groom's father	Chief usher	Usher	Usher
Jacket and trousers							
Waistcoat							
Shirt							
Tie or cravat							
Cufflinks (if necessary)							
Gloves							
Top hat							
Shoes							
Socks							

Gifts

Jot down the names of those you will be buying gifts for so you can make sure no one is left out.

Role	Name	Gift
Bride		
Best man		
Chief Usher		
Usher		
Usher		
Chief bridesmaid		
Bridesmaid		
Bridesmaid		
Bridesmaid		
Flower girl		
Pageboy		
Pageboy		
Bride's parents		
Groom's parents		

The groom's budget sheets

The first pages here will help you work out your household budget. The remaining pages relate to the wedding planning, and not only tell you who is usually expected to pay for the various items, but also give you space to jot down all your outlays. Make sure you budget for all the bits and pieces as well as the major items – it's easy to let things run away.

Household income and expenditure

Having some idea of your budget for married life is good advance planning. Needless to say, if there's more going out than coming in, then something needs to be done!

Source of income	Income	Details	£ per month	£ per year
Husband	Salary			
	Interest from savings, etc.			
Wife	Salary			
	Interest from savings, etc.			
Other income				
Total				

Type of expenditure	Expense	Details	£ per month	£ per year
Home	Mortgage/Rent			
	Council tax			
	Insurance	Life		
		Building		
		Contents		
	Loan repayments			
	Water			
	Gas			
	Electricity			
	Telephone			
	Maintenance			
	Improvements			
Travelling	Car	Tax		
		Insurance		
		MOT		
		Maintenance		
		Fuel		
	Public transport			
	Loan repayments			

The groom

Type of expenditure	Expense	Details	£ per month	£ per year
Housekeeping	Food			
	Cleaning			
Personal	Clothing			
	Accessories			
	Cosmetics			
Medical	Doctor			
	Dentist			
	Insurance			
Leisure	Entertainment			
	Gifts			
	Parties			
	TV licence			
Holidays				
Savings				
Pension				
Total				

Wedding clothes

This section tells you who usually pays for what, but remember not all weddings are the same, so clarify each item before you start.

Expense	Item	Traditional payer	Payer	Estimate £	Actual £
Bride	Wedding dress and accessories	Bride's family			
	Going-away outfit	Bride's family			
Bridesmaids	Outfits	Bride's family			
Pageboys	Outfits	Bride's family			
Groom	Wedding suit and accessories	Groom			
	Going-away outfit	Groom			
Best man	Suit, shirt and tie	Groom's family if hired			
	Shoes and accessories	Best man			
Ushers	Suit, shirt and tie	Groom's family if hired			
	Shoes and accessories	Ushers			
Bride's father	Suit, shirt and tie	Bride's family			
	Accessories	Bride's father			
Groom's father	Outfit	Groom's father			

Transport

The ushers are responsible for their own transport, as is the best man. The bride's attendants are on their own once they are at the reception. Although traditionally the bride's parents are responsible for getting the groom's parents to the reception, in practice this doesn't always make much sense as they have to go separately to the church and home from the reception.

Expense	Item	Traditional payer	Payer	Estimate £	Actual £
Transport to ceremony	Bride and her father	Bride's family			
	Bride's mother and attendants	Bride's family			
	Groom and best man	Groom's family			
Transport to reception	Bride and groom	Groom's family			
	Bride's attendants	Bride's family			
	Bride's parents	Bride's family			
	Groom's parents	Bride's family			
Transport from reception	Bride and groom	Groom's family			
Decoration	Ribbons for the cars	Groom's family			
	Old boots, etc.	Best man			

Flowers

Expense	Item	Traditional payer	Payer	Estimate £	Actual £
Flowers for ceremony	Bride's bouquet	Groom's family			
	Bride's headdress	Groom's family			
	Ceremony venue	Bride's family			
	Bridesmaids' and flower girls' posies and headdresses	Groom's family			
	Pageboys' buttonholes	Groom's family			
	Buttonholes for groom, best man, ushers and fathers	Groom's family			
	Corsages for mothers	Groom's family			
	Dried-flower keepsake	Groom's family			
Flowers for reception	Table settings, etc.	Bride's family			

Ceremony fees
This is very much the groom's territory.

Expense	Item	Traditional payer	Payer	Estimate £	Actual £
Ceremony	Minister or registrar	Groom			
	Banns or marriage certificate	Groom			
	Verger	Groom			
	Organist	Groom			
	Choir	Groom			
	Soloist or singers	Groom			
	Bell-ringers	Groom			
	Personal donation	Groom			
	Collection	Groom			
Miscellaneous	Petty cash for the best man on the day	Groom			

Reception

This was traditionally paid for by the bride's family, but often nowadays the groom's parents contribute to the costs. If guests are staying overnight after the reception, they are usually responsible for their own costs, although the relevant family may wish to contribute.

Expense	Item	Traditional payer	Payer	Estimate £	Actual £
Reception	Venue	Bride's family			
	Food	Bride's family			
	Drinks	Bride's family			
	Entertainment	Bride's family			
	Insurance	Bride's family			

Honeymoon

Expense	Item	Traditional payer	Payer	Estimate £	Actual £
Travel	Flights, etc.	Groom			
	Passports, visas, etc.	Groom			
Accommodation	Hotels, etc.	Groom			
Miscellaneous	Maps and guide books	Groom			
Medical	Inoculations	Groom			
Clothes and accessories	Bride	Bride			
	Groom	Groom			

Gifts and parties

Obviously, you buy the ring and the present for the bride, and she buys your ring and present.

Expense	Item	Traditional payer	Payer	Estimate £	Actual £
Gifts	For the bridesmaids	Groom			
	For the pageboys	Bride			
	For the best man	Groom			
	For the ushers	Groom			
	For the bride's parents	Bride and groom			
	For the groom's parents	Bride and groom			
Parties	Engagement	Bride's family			
	Rehearsal	Bride's family			
	Hen night	Bride			
	Stag night	Groom			

Anniversaries

Looking forward a little, this is perhaps a good moment to mention anniversaries. Most people like to celebrate their wedding anniversary – and forgetting it altogether is a seriously bad move! Apart from anything else, it's a good time to take stock of all the good things about your marriage, and remind yourselves of all the great things you have in store together.

Silver (25), Pearl (30), Ruby (40), Golden (50) and Diamond (60) are the really special dates.

How can I make sure I don't forget?

Use whatever methods you usually do to remind you of important things. Imagine the boss has asked you for an interview to review your salary and give you a 20 per cent rise – you wouldn't forget that, and this is far more important.

Write it in your diary, making a note at the end of the year to put it in next year's diary. Input it into your personal organiser. Ask your mum or your best mate to remind you if they are better than you at that kind of thing. Do anything and everything you can think of, but **don't forget**.

What should I buy for our wedding anniversaries?

Wedding anniversaries are usually associated with a particular type of material or metal – paper, silk, silver, and so on. The actual materials are based on the fact that the bride would bring everything she needed for her new home, and this was the order in which they would wear out and need to be replaced. That may be very sensible, but don't forget that you are reminding yourselves of the happiest and most romantic day of your lives, so being sensible may not be your top priority. Try to apply a bit of imagination to get something that she will really enjoy.

☺ Ask yourself what you would prefer: a CD collection of your favourite artist or a heated towel rail? Apply the same principles to what you choose for your wife and go for the personal touch: a weekend in Paris or a silk negligée sounds much more appealing to me than a four-slice toaster.

A husband often gives his wife an eternity ring on the birth of their first child, or at another significant event such as a special anniversary.

The few ideas below are just to set you thinking. If you know she would appreciate and enjoy practical things for the home, the choice is easy; if not, maybe this will give you some food for thought. If all else fails, revert to jewellery, or champagne, flowers and Belgian chocolates.

Anniversary year	Traditional association	Gift ideas
1	Cotton	Attach a cotton thread to her anniversary card and make her follow it round the house to find her present
2	Paper	Tickets for the theatre or a West End show
3	Leather or straw	A leather jacket or handbag (forget the straw unless she likes horse riding, in which case buy tickets for a horse-riding event)
4	Silk or flowers	Silk underwear
5	Wood	A garden swing (with two seats) or a rose arbour
6	Sugar or iron	A trip to a restaurant renowned for its splendid desserts
7	Wool or copper	An Armani suit (well, sometimes you have to push your luck)
8	Bronze	A trip to a sculpture museum
9	Pottery	A course of pottery evening classes for both of you or a candlelit dinner followed by a private viewing of *Ghost* (if you haven't seen it, there's a great pottery scene).
10	Tin	A weekend in Cornwall with a tour round a tin mine
11	Steel	A CD of steel band music or a De Lorean car
12	Silk and fine linen	A designer outfit
13	Lace	Lingerie

Anniversary year	Traditional association	Gift ideas
14	Ivory	A piano, or tickets for a piano recital or concert
15	Crystal	Cut-glass champagne flutes – and the champagne
20	China	An antique china ornament
25	Silver	Jewellery or silver items
30	Pearl	Pearl earrings and a meal at the nearest oyster bar
35	Coral	A trip to the Great Barrier Reef
40	Ruby	A case of vintage red wine or port
45	Sapphire	A cruise to the Caribbean where the sea is sapphire blue
50	Gold	An appointment with a goldsmith to commission a unique piece of jewellery
55	Emerald	A trip to Ireland
60	Diamond	A diamond ring or necklace
70	Platinum	Jewellery
75	Second diamond	Diamond earrings

Chapter 2
The Best Man

For 'best man', read 'best mate'. Your job is to be in the right place at the right time and generally help out the groom, get him to the church on time, keep the rings safe, reassure him when he's nervous, oversee the ushers, make sure the guests get safely to the reception and act as toastmaster. And that's just for starters.

You'll need to chat through all the specifics beforehand with the groom, and probably the bride as well, as different couples will expect a different input from their right-hand man. In general, the more formal the wedding, the more formal your role is likely to be.

You are probably the groom's brother or best friend. Some grooms these days choose a female best man, although that's still pretty rare. If you are that unusual kind of best man, please forgive the use of the male pronoun throughout this chapter.

☺ A female best man must be very careful about what she wears so that there's no danger that she outshines the bride. Communicate with the bride early to make sure you hit the right style and level of formality.

Do I get an invitation?

The groom should ask you personally whether you will be his best man, but you'll still receive an invitation from the hosts, usually the bride's parents, and the normal rules of courtesy apply. Don't assume that as you are the best man, they know you are coming; send a reply. Respond within three days in the same degree of formality as the invitation. If the invitation is in the third person, then you reply in the third person (and there's no need to sign). Otherwise, a simple note of acknowledgement and acceptance is all it needs.

☺ You know that 'RSVP' means *'Répondez s'il vous plaît'* (in other words, reply) – so make sure you do!

What do I have to do?

Fortunately for you, most of the planning work is done by everyone else, but the more you know about what they have put together, the more you'll be able to help out and ensure that the rest of the wedding party have a trouble-free and enjoyable day. These are the jobs you are usually expected to do.

- Arrange the stag night.
- Look after the groom's outfit before the wedding and return it afterwards, if hired, along with your own and those of the other members of the wedding party.
- Buy your own outfit if it's not hired.

- Attend the rehearsal of the ceremony.
- Take responsibility for the groom's documents and money and the ring(s) and hand them over at the appropriate time.
- Get the groom to the church on time.
- Make sure the buttonholes and corsages and the order of service sheets are at the church for the ushers to distribute.
- Oversee the ushers, making sure they know their jobs and do them.
- If there are no ushers, you also fulfil their role.
- Organise the transport and parking at the church and reception.
- Pay the church fees.
- Sign the register as a witness, if requested.
- Help the photographer to organise the photos.
- Join the reception receiving line to welcome the guests.
- Take charge of the display of gifts and make sure it is safe.
- Act as master of ceremonies at the reception, if there is no official toastmaster.
- Make a speech and read telemessages, telegrams, cards and e-mails.
- Dance with the chief bridesmaid.
- Circulate at the reception and help ensure that the guests are enjoying themselves.
- Supervise the decoration of the get-away car.

There may be other jobs you'll be expected to do, which will vary depending on the circumstances. Discussion in advance and willingness on the day are all most of it takes. However, it is vital that you know what is expected of you so you can do everything well and make sure nothing has been overlooked. If, for example, the bride thinks you are picking up the buttonholes from her house to take to the church, while you also need to be somewhere else at the same time to pick up the groom, that's a recipe for trouble. If you find out in good time, you can deputise your ushers, or other willing helpers, to fill in the gaps.

> ➤ The bride and groom should organise a meeting, often with the chief bridesmaid, to go through the details of what they would like you to do. If they don't, organise it yourself. It will be to everyone's benefit.

Is that all?!
You'll need a long list of skills as well: organisation, confidence, calmness, diplomacy, authority, tact, punctuality, thoughtfulness, a sociable disposition, common sense, voice projection, sobriety ... but don't worry – all you really need is the common sense to read this book and do a bit of planning.

> ➤ Remember that the day is all about helping your best mate to have a wonderful time. He has asked you because it's important to him that you share in his big day. Being there and being you is what matters – as long as you are sober and house-trained, of course.

You'll find a list of what happens on the day starting on page 235. Read it through so you know what to expect and you'll feel much more comfortable about the whole thing.

Make a list of all the jobs that you have to do and when you have to do them. Look at each one in relation to what you know you are good at – and where you see a gap, plug it! Make sure you know where your weaknesses lie too. If, for example, you know you only remember things once you have written them in your diary, write them in your diary. If it's several months ahead and they haven't printed the next year's diaries yet, jot the dates down at the back of your existing diary to be transferred as soon as possible. If your ten-decibel alarm clock never wakes you up, use whatever drastic measures are necessary: for example, give your neighbour a door key and a bucket of water. If you know that you'll reach for the Dutch courage when your nerve starts to fail, practise mixing a powerful but alcohol-free cocktail and have some ready on the big day (if necessary, have someone on hand to pour it for you too). If you feel you're not very good at chatting to people you don't know, start making a list of things you can say to perfect strangers to start a conversation (see page 150).

The big terror, of course, is the speech, but even that is not beyond you. Planning is the key here, so see the guide on pages 217–34. In the meantime, just remind yourself:

- It's only about four minutes. That's not very long.
- The guests want you to succeed and they all want to have a good time, so they are not a critical audience.
- You don't have to be a stand-up comic.
- People expect sincerity; this is your best mate's wedding so you can easily do that.

☺ It's an honour to be asked to be a best man, and you **can** do it! But if you really believe it's beyond you and you'd ruin the day, say so in plenty of time so that the groom has the maximum time to find a replacement. If he's your mate, he should understand if you feel you just can't go through with it.

Who helps me out?

A wedding is not a competition; everyone helps everyone else, and there'll be both families to muck in and make sure everything gets done. In the preparation stages, the groom should make sure you have all the information you need to do your job. If he doesn't, ask him for it. If he still doesn't, or if he's forgotten what day of the week it is, go straight to the bride. She's the kingpin of the operation after all and will have the final say. When it comes to carrying out your duties, your main supporters are the ushers.

Usher! Usher! We all fall down ...

Hopefully not, as the ushers are your official helpers. The groom may involve you in choosing a few men to help out with various jobs, although it is usually a foregone conclusion: brothers of the bride or groom or a few close friends.

The ushers make sure all the wedding party have their buttonholes and corsages. They distribute the order of service sheets to the guests as they arrive at the church and escort them to their seats. If photos are not allowed in the church, they discreetly mention this to anyone wielding a camera or camcorder. After the service, they help you to make sure everyone has transport to the reception, and the chief usher should be the last to leave, making sure there are no stray guests, top hats or gloves left in the church or register office. Read through their chapter to familiarise yourself with what their jobs are.

If there are no ushers, that's all down to you as well, so perhaps you could ask a friend to help out if you know you are expected to be doing more than one thing at any one time.

What do I wear?

This is up to the bride and groom, as you'll dress with the same degree of formality as the groom (making sure that you don't outshine him, of course!). Firstly, find out whether the outfits are to be hired, whether it's morning dress or lounge suits, and so on.

> ☺ Things like the colour scheme of the wedding party are important to brides, so don't think it won't matter if you wear your Winnie-the-Pooh waistcoat without asking. It almost certainly will.

If it is a formal wedding, it will be a morning suit and top hat (see page 71), and if the suits are to be hired, you'll have to go along to fittings with the groom. Make sure you know when to collect your suit. It will be up to you to sort out shirt, socks, shoes and so on at your own expense. If you don't know what's expected, **ask**. You'll certainly need to know if the bride has a colour scheme in mind for things like formal handkerchiefs or waistcoats. By the way, you don't actually have to wear your hat and gloves. Hold the gloves in your left hand and hold the hat by the brim.

> ➤ Don't forget that formal shirts will need cufflinks.

For an informal wedding, it's even more important to know what the bride and groom have in mind so that you can buy or choose an outfit accordingly. It's a good idea to go shopping for your outfit with the groom, then there won't be any misunderstandings. In this scenario, you will be responsible for the cost of your entire outfit.

> ➤ Have a private dress rehearsal with the groom a week or so before the wedding to make sure you have thought of all the details: cufflinks, hankies, the right colour socks, and so on. Take off all the labels from new clothes, peel off the price stickers from the bottom of your shoes and wear them just enough to make sure they are comfortable and the soles are slightly scratched and not slippery. Check that belts are the correct width and length.

After the wedding, you will be responsible for collecting the groom's suit from wherever he has changed into his going-away clothes, and returning it if it has been hired. Make sure you know where he will be leaving it when he gets changed, and where and when it has to be returned. Return your own suit at the same time, and make sure that those belonging to the other members of the wedding party have also been returned.

Who's who?

You are part of the wedding party – the most important guests and family members. Find out the names of all the others and jot them down on your checklist (see page 165). Be especially sure to find out the names and relationships of partners if any of the parents or guests are divorced.

> ☺ Take the bridesmaids out for a drink – or a McDonald's if this is more appropriate – so that they all know one another.

First things first – what about the stag night?

You are in charge of organising a good send-off for the groom, but you should really do this in discussion with him, so take charge early and make sure it all gets put together. Don't let the groom leave it all to the last minute. Once you know the wedding date, you can set the date for the stag night the week before. Weekends are generally best as it's easier for people to travel and it gives them plenty of time to recover.

> ☺ Reassure the bride that you have booked the stag night well in advance of the wedding, and that arrangements have been made to get the groom home safely in one piece (it's best if it's all true, too).

Ask the groom what he fancies doing (see the list of ideas on pages 90–2) and plan out the evening. Think about whether people have to travel a distance to attend, or whether everyone you're expecting lives locally. It will make a difference to what you decide to do. If some people are coming from out of town, where are they going to stay?

- Where will you all meet up?
- What time will you meet?
- Where are you going?
- How many of you are there?
- Do you need to book anywhere?
- Do you need to arrange transport?
- Where is everyone sleeping?

Ask the groom who he wants to invite. The usual list includes the bride's and groom's fathers and brothers, the ushers, and the groom's best friends, past and present. Get their names and addresses and get in touch by letter, by phone or by e-mail, whatever is appropriate. Ask them to confirm whether or not they can come, so you have exact numbers and no one is left waiting at the station for you to pick them up.

➤ The fathers usually leave early, so you might want to work that thought into your plans for the evening ... and theirs ...

Traditionally the groom used to pay for the stag night but that's unusual now so most guests will be expected to pay something towards the evening. Sometimes the groom will pay for a meal, or entry to a club and the guests will pay the rest. It's important that you know what the groom is paying for and work out how much you think the evening will cost the guests. Let them know in advance so there's no embarrassment.

☺ Don't play any jokes that won't seem funny the next morning (so leave the hairclippers at home) and don't book a stripper if the groom doesn't want one.

This is your chance to test your speechmaking skills in a relaxed environment, and bring out all those comments and jokes that you certainly should not use on the wedding day, such as recollections of previous girlfriends, or the groom's less attractive personal habits!

Don't drive, and don't let the groom drive. Walk (or stagger), have the phone numbers of local taxi firms, or hire a minibus with a driver for the evening. Whatever suits the occasion is fine, but **plan it in advance.** Since you are in charge of making the evening a success and making sure everyone – especially the groom – gets home safely, try not to get too smashed yourself.

What's this about a rehearsal?

The minister sometimes arranges a rehearsal a week or so before the wedding to run through the service. Use this opportunity to meet all the wedding party, clear up any queries you may still have, and to give your gift to the bride and groom.

In any event, you should have read through the outline of what is going to happen on the day, and marked your special responsibilities (see pages 235–41). It's reassuring to make sure you know where everything is and to run through what will happen. If you know you don't remember things, jot them down. If you're not sure, ask.

☺ Superstition says that it's good luck for the bride to meet a chimney sweep 'in his blacks'. Persuade a friend to dress up and greet the bride when she arrives at church, but make sure he doesn't go too close!

You can also use the rehearsal as an opportunity to familiarise yourself with the ceremony venue. Check out the parking and where the photos are being taken.

➤ If it's a double wedding, the two best men should get together to plan and share out the jobs. The senior groom's best man takes precedence.

How should I organise transport?

You and the groom have to organise the transport, so talk to him about what he wants you to do, whether you are actually doing any of the booking or arranging, or making any of the payments.

The ushers and guests should arrange their own transport to the church and to the reception, so you should only need to check that they have made suitable arrangements and that no one is stranded. However, it is a good idea to ask the bride if she would like you to organise a lift for any particular guests who may have a transport problem – elderly aunts, etc.

> ☺ Send a text message to the bride on the morning of the wedding to reassure her that all the plans are in place to get the groom to the church on time.

You obviously have to organise transport to get yourself and the groom to the church on time. You'll also have to be among the last to leave the reception too, as one of your last jobs is making sure everyone has transport home.

> ➤ It's a good idea to have a trial run of the route to the church a few weeks in advance on the same day of the week and at the same time, to check that there aren't any particular traffic problems.

If you intend to act as driver, check out the car you will be using. If it's your own, take a long look at it. It may be your pride and joy, but does it look good? More importantly, is it reliable? If the answer to either of these is No, think again. Once you have decided on the right car, get down to preparing both the car and you, the driver, for the big day.

- Have the car serviced.
- If you are borrowing a car, make sure you are insured to drive it.
- Clean it inside and out the day before.
- Fill it up with petrol.
- Buy ribbons if you are going to decorate it.
- Decide on which route you are going to take.
- Find out exactly where you are going to park it at the church.
- Find out if there are any carnivals, road works or anything else that might cause a hold-up on the day.
- Decide exactly what time you will need to leave home to get to the church on time (have a practice run, if necessary).

> ➤ Have the numbers of a couple of local taxis firms just in case. Programme them into your mobile phone.

What do I do at the ceremony?

You get the groom to the church well before the ceremony is due to start, have a few pictures taken, then wait with him in the front right-hand pew until the bride arrives. Once the music strikes up, you both step forward. When the minister asks for the rings, you give them to him. After the vows, hymns, prayers and address, you'll go with the wedding party to the vestry and sign the register if you have been asked to be one of the witnesses. You then offer your arm to the chief bridesmaid and escort her out of the church, following the bride and groom. You help to organise the guests for the photos, then get everyone to the reception.

That last bit will probably not be as simple as it sounds, so make sure you have it all well planned. Check out the ushers' duties in advance. You must agree whether you are leaving the church with the wedding party to join the receiving line and leaving the ushers to organise transport, or whether you are staying until last.

The bride and groom will obviously go from the church to the reception in the main wedding car. You may be asked to transport the bridesmaids, in which case you will definitely need ribbons on the car, or some of the other wedding guests. Find out in advance whom you are driving.

It's your job to make sure no one is left stranded at church. If there are ushers, delegate that job to the chief usher so you can get to the reception. Ask him to check inside the church for lost property as well as outside for lost guests before he leaves.

☺ Prepare a supply of cards with your mobile number on so that anyone who gets stuck en route to the reception can ring you for help. Make sure you have the ushers' mobile numbers.

Once you get to the reception, make sure the bride and groom's car is parked at the reception venue ready for them to leave on their honeymoon. Make sure it is parked safely and that all the honeymoon cases are packed in the car – preferably in the boot where they can't be seen. Keep the keys in a safe place and don't forget where that safe place is.

What should I check at the reception venue?
Since a lot of your job is at the reception, it's a good idea to go along to the venue with the bride and groom and check that everything is well organised. You'll welcome guests in the receiving line, possibly act as toastmaster (see page 148), make your own speech, and sort out the gifts, the changing facilities for the bride and groom, and the get-away car and luggage.

Usually the best man joins the receiving line to greet the guests. You stand at the end after the bride, groom and their parents. Once all the guests have arrived, you should circulate and help to ensure that everyone has a drink and someone to talk to.

Make sure that a table is placed by the receiving line. There are bound to be some guests who bring gifts with them, so they will need somewhere they can deposit them before greeting the wedding party. Find someone to be responsible for keeping the gifts safe (again, this may be you), choose a suitable place for them and make sure all the gifts are placed there and not forgotten.

> ➤ Young guests can be delegated to help carry the gifts to a secure room. They'll enjoy the responsibility.

When it is time for the meal, you or the toastmaster will ask people to sit down. Find out what the seating plan is for the meal. Will the bride organise a copy of the plan so you and the ushers can help people to their seats? Will there be place names? You'll have a designated spot on the top table.

Chief bridesmaid	Groom's father	Bride's mother	Groom	Bride	Bride's father	Groom's mother	Best man

The speeches are usually made after dessert. Find out the order of the speeches, who is making each speech and what the facilities are like. Is there a microphone system? How does it work? Who is introducing the speakers? (Is it you?) How long is your speech expected to be? (There's lots more on this starting on page 217.)

> ☺ Prepare some videos or set up games to keep the youngsters amused, or find them some jobs handing out drinks or nibbles to keep them busy. Ask your ushers to help out with ideas and on the day.

Find out what will happen after the meal so you can tell the guests. For example, if all the tables are being cleared away, you can ask them to congregate in another room, or at one end of the hall, for example, until everything is set up for the disco/band/etc. For the first dance, the bride and groom take the floor alone. About halfway through the dance, the groom's father joins them with the bride's mother, and the bride's father with the groom's mother. You then invite the chief bridesmaid on to the floor. After that, it's a free-for-all!

> ☺ Put a good cassette tape or a few dance CDs in the boot of your car with a portable player. Hopefully it'll stay there, but if there are any problems with the sound system, you could be the one to save the day.

You should bring the clothes for the groom to change into to the reception venue and have them somewhere safe where he can change at the end of the party, then take charge of his suit. You'll also see to the get-away car and luggage.

What does a toastmaster do?
At large, formal weddings there'll be a professional toastmaster whose job is to announce loudly and clearly when it's time for something to be done. At a medium-sized formal wedding, that may be you, although since you'll be part of the receiving line, you escape that bit! Here are the crucial points.

- As the guests approach the receiving line, you quietly ask their full names, then announce them as they approach to shake hands with the wedding party.

  Mr and Mrs John Jones: This is the correct way of addressing a husband and wife.

  Mr Michael Turner and Mrs Elizabeth Knight: Announce mixed couples together only if they present themselves to you together. If they come to you individually, announce them individually as below.

  Mr John Green: Straightforward – but don't forget the Mr.

  Mrs Peter Smith: This is how you should announce a married woman attending without her husband, but if she tells you 'Mrs Mary Smith', then use the form she suggests. (She may be widowed or divorced or simply prefer to use her own name.)

- When it is time for the meal: 'Ladies and gentlemen, pray (or please) be seated; dinner is now being served'.
- When everyone is seated: 'Ladies and gentlemen, pray be silent for grace' or 'Ladies and gentlemen, the Reverend – (give his/her name) will now say grace'. (If the minister is not present, the bride's father will say grace.)
- Before the speeches and toasts, make sure the guests' glasses are full.
- Make sure the microphones are working.
- Introduce the speakers.
- Announce the cutting of the cake.
- Announce the programme for the rest of the reception.

What about the speeches?

This is the part that best men dread the most. It's only a tiny part of the day, but probably the one with the most impact – certainly the most impact on your nerves – so we've given it a whole chapter to itself to make sure you are well prepared and it all goes perfectly. Turn to page 217 for the full treatment.

Keeping the party going

It's a great help at the reception if you keep a general eye out for anyone standing on their own and bring them back into the party. If you don't find it easy to talk to strangers, take a look at these start-up ideas and follow-up questions, personalise them, add some more of your own, and you'll always have something to say. Try to ask open questions that encourage people to give you more than a 'Yes' or 'No' answer.

- I'm Peter (or whoever), the best man, it's nice to meet you. I don't think we've met.
- What relation are you to the bride/groom?
- I expect you've known her/him since you were babies?
- I expect you have some interesting anecdotes about when she/he was small.
- Doesn't the bride look lovely. Do you know where she bought the dress?
- Have you known them a long time?
- Where did you meet them first?
- Did you have far to travel?
- Do you know anything about their honeymoon destination?
- Did you enjoy the meal? I thought the (whatever) was particularly good.
- Are there any relatives/friends here you haven't seen for a long time?

How should I decorate the get-away car?
The ancient tradition of attaching old boots to the get-away car stems from the time when the bride's father presented the groom with one of her slippers, giving the groom 'the upper hand', which entitled him to thrash his wife should she displease him! The slipper was placed at the head of the bed on the husband's side to remind the wife who was boss. However, if

the wife assumed the dominant role, neighbours transferred 'the power of the slipper' to her and named her 'the old boot'!

Collect together some old tin cans, balloons, ribbons, and so on to tie on to the car. Make a 'Just Married' sign and take along some string or cord to fix it on and some confetti to sprinkle in the glove box. Recruit the chief bridesmaid or a few friends and slip away while the reception is in full swing to decorate the going-away car.

> ☺ Put a little cleaning-up kit on the back seat for the bride and groom to use the next day, or when they arrive at their destination: a pair of scissors, a few cloths, or anything you think may be useful.

Don't let anyone tamper with the car's mechanics or use shaving foam or lipstick on the paintwork (they leave indelible marks). Make sure all the windows are left clear so that the driver can still see all around.

What about a present?
You most definitely do buy a wedding gift for the bride and groom, and since you are someone special, try to make it something unique and personal.

Think about what the couple would really appreciate.
- Do they want household things if they are setting up home?
- If so, what's the colour scheme in their home?

- Would they rather have something personal they can keep, such as a photograph frame, a picture or an ornament?
- Would they like something more unusual like a balloon trip or tickets for a show or an event?

Photos and videos

After the ceremony, and possibly at the reception, the photographer will have a list of shots he has arranged to take of the wedding guests: bride and groom, groom with best man, bride's family, the happy couple with their parents, and so on. If you can be on stand-by to help the photographer herd people into shot, that will help make the process quicker and more painless. Have a chat with the bride in advance and ask her for a list of photos if she wants you to help.

What else can I do to help?

You know the set-up better than anyone, but if you can offer some support in any way it will be much appreciated.

- If you know the budget is tight, and you have a PC, you could offer to do a seating plan on it, or even print the invitations or order of service sheets.
- Offer to accommodate any guests who are travelling a long distance.
- Bring along a video for the children to watch while the tables are being cleared. (Make sure it's appropriate to the age group!)

- Offer to help the bride's mother with her after-wedding tasks, such as sending out slices of cake to those who were unable to attend on the day, collecting and processing photo orders from those who want prints.

☺ One old superstition says that a new broom and a loaf of bread should be at the newlyweds' home before they arrive. A jar of pennies may also be left in the kitchen for good luck.

While the couple are away on honeymoon, you could keep an eye on the house and feed any pets for them. You could buy some bread and milk the day before they get back – or, better still, put a bottle of wine in the fridge – or decorate the house with some flowers or balloons.

☺ Offer the couple a lift from the airport when they return.

The best man's diary

Six months before
- ❑ Enter the wedding date in your diary.
- ❑ Cancel any other engagements for that date and the preceding couple of days.
- ❑ Talk to the bride and groom about what you are expected to do.
- ❑ Help to choose the ushers.

Three months before
- ❑ Discuss plans with the bride, groom and chief bridesmaid.
- ❑ Consult and return the wedding gift list; buy something special, a gift card and wrapping paper. Keep the receipt in case you need to exchange if someone duplicates it.
- ❑ Have a meeting with the wedding party members so you all know who's who.
- ❑ Brief the ushers on what is expected of them.
- ❑ Buy or arrange your hired outfit and accessories.
- ❑ Check that the groom and the ushers have organised their own outfits and accessories.

Two months before
- ❑ Send a written reply to the invitation within three days of receipt (see page 174). Remember the bride's mother holds the list, so telling the groom you'll be there isn't enough.

- ❑ Find out who is making a speech, the order of the speeches and whether the bride wants to you thank anyone special.
- ❑ Write, time and practise your speech.
- ❑ Organise and book the stag night for a week before the wedding.
- ❑ Check that all the transport bookings have been made.
- ❑ Visit the ceremony venue and check the parking arrangements.
- ❑ Visit the reception venue with the bride and groom to check on parking, changing facilities and gift storage.
- ❑ Get a copy of the seating plans for the ceremony and reception and give a copy to the ushers.
- ❑ Get your mum to teach you the steps to the waltz.
- ❑ Keep in touch with the groom and offer any help and support that's needed.

One month before
- ❑ Check that buttonholes have been ordered and confirm the arrangements for collection.
- ❑ Finalise transport for you and the groom to the church.
- ❑ Do a timed run from the groom's home to the ceremony venue.
- ❑ Find out if there are likely to be special traffic problems on the actual day, for example carnivals, road works or a road race.

❏ Finalise transport for yourself to reception and home afterwards. Are you driving anyone else?
❏ Buy ribbons for the car.
❏ Check the arrangements for the newly-weds' get-away car to be parked at the reception.

Two weeks before

❏ Finalise your speech. Make two copies and keep them safe.
❏ Check with the bride if any special transport arrangements are required.
❏ Ask the bride for a copy of the list of photos to be taken so that you've an idea of what's expected.
❏ Make sure you have emergency telephone numbers for taxi firms.
❏ Warn the ushers of any parking or traffic problems and make suitable arrangements.
❏ Prepare a back-up system of appropriate music that'll appeal to all generations just in case.
❏ Prepare some videos or games to keep the younger guests amused.

One week before

❏ Deliver your gift to the bride at her parents' home.
❏ Check that the groom has the ring.
❏ Check that the licence/banns certificate has been collected.

❑ Check that the groom has all necessary documents for the wedding and honeymoon.
❑ Confirm all car hire bookings and/or taxi arrangements.
❑ Buy a cheap spare ring, just in case.
❑ Buy/acquire get-away car decorations – paper streamers, balloons, empty drinks cans, Christmas decorations.
❑ Attend stag night and see the groom home safely.
❑ Collect hired outfits for you and groom if appropriate.
❑ Check your outfit and try everything on.
❑ Have a hair cut.
❑ Attend the dress rehearsal.

The day before
❑ Set your alarm and arrange alarm calls.
❑ Clean the car, fill with petrol, check water and oil levels.
❑ Charge up your mobile phone.
❑ Collect the order of service sheets.
❑ Double-check arrangements for collecting the buttonholes.
❑ Run through the list of what is going to happen on the day (see pages 235–41).
❑ Pack your own bag of essentials:
   ❑ Mobile/phone card
   ❑ Cash for telephone and spending
   ❑ Emergency numbers
   ❑ Spare name cards
   ❑ Spare order of service sheets

❑ Speech cards
❑ Decorations for going-away car
❑ Umbrella
❑ Aspirin
❑ Rescue remedy or calming aromatherapy gel
❑ Cigarettes and hip flask for last-minute panics!
❑ Good luck mascot

❑ Have an early, alcohol-free night so that you're not fighting a hangover throughout the ceremony.

On the day

This is not really a day for ticking boxes, but make sure you do all of these before you set off.

❑ Ring the groom to check that he has ready:
  ❑ Outfit and accessories
  ❑ Certificate of banns or marriage licence
  ❑ Tickets, passports, visas, etc.
  ❑ Church fees
  ❑ Ring(s)
  ❑ Cases packed and loaded (if not done previously)
  ❑ Car keys
  ❑ Any telemessages, telegrams, cards and e-mails that may have arrived at the groom's house
  ❑ Cash for the day
❑ Tie ribbons on car(s).

❑ Make sure the bride's and groom's luggage and the cleaning-up kit are packed in the get-away car, fill it with petrol and park it at reception venue.

❑ Collect the buttonholes, corsages and order of service sheets (the flowers will probably be at the bride's home, the sheets with whoever has had them printed).

❑ Ring the ushers to remind them to be on time and check through their duties.

❑ Ring the bride's parents and wish them well.

❑ Text or ring the bride to reassure her that everything is under control.

Set out for the groom's home early. Take the rings, church fees and documentation from him, then set off for the ceremony.

➤ We've provided a separate run-through starting on page 160 of everything that happens on the big day itself once you have arrived at the church.

After the wedding

❑ Check that all gifts are safely stored.

❑ Return hired outfits and check that the ushers have returned theirs.

❑ Send a thank you note for any gifts you have received.

❑ Return any deposits to the groom and pass on cleaning bills.

The best man on the day

This is your run-through of all the likely events. Personalise it and read it through several times so you know what to expect.

At the church

- Arrive at the church with the groom and have some photos taken.
- Pay the church fees (or do this later in the vestry after the register is signed).
- Hand over banns certificate from the groom's church.
- Take your seats in the front pew on the right-hand side.
- Switch your mobile phone to **silent**.
- Take charge of the groom's hat and gloves.

> ➤ If the bride is very late, **go outside** and ring the bride's home or the car-hire company to find out why.

- The music changes tempo when the bride is about to enter. Stand up and take a step forward, standing on the right side of and a little behind the groom.
- Move forward with the groom to stand in front of the steps.
- Hand over the ring(s) when asked to do so, then step back and take your original place for the rest of the ceremony.

- When the bride and groom are ready to go to the vestry to sign the register, pick up your own and the groom's hat and gloves, offer your left arm to the chief bridesmaid and follow the bride and groom.
- Sign the register if asked to do so.
- Check that male members of the wedding party have their hats and gloves.
- Offer your arm again to the chief bridesmaid and follow the bride and groom out of the church.
- Help the photographer to position guests for the photographs.
- Escort the bride and groom to their car on time.
- Ensure that ushers are making sure that all guests have transport to the reception.
- Leave for the reception with the bridesmaids after the bride and groom and parents or, if there are no ushers, stay behind to ensure that no one's left stranded.

At the reception
At a very formal reception, a professional toastmaster will announce guests as they approach the receiving line and you will join the end of the receiving line with the chief bridesmaid. If there is no toastmaster, you take on his duties.

If you are not in the receiving line, welcome guests and encourage them to leave any gifts on a table positioned before the receiving line so that they have their hands free to shake hands.

- Receive, take charge and ensure the safety of wedding gifts.
- Collect all the telemessages, telegrams, cards or e-mails from the bride's father and reception desk and vet them so that you don't read anything unsuitable. If there are many with the same sentiments such as 'best wishes for the future', read the sentiment once and list the senders' names.
- Offer drinks to guests or circulate and be hospitable!
- Once the meal is ready, announce it (unless there is a toastmaster).
- Help the guests find their places on the seating plan.
- Escort guests to their seats.
- Take your seat at the top table.
- Request silence for grace (unless there is a toastmaster). The bride's father may say grace if the minister is absent.
- After the last course, introduce the speakers (if there's no toastmaster).

☺ Have some thoughts ready so you can improvise a speech or a few ad libs if any of the speakers dries up or has too much to drink.

- Make your speech, read telemessages, telegrams, cards and e-mails.
- Propose the toast to the newly-weds.

- Announce the cake-cutting ceremony if there's no toastmaster: 'Ladies and gentlemen, may I have your attention please? The bride and groom will now cut the cake.'
- Once this is done, announce the programme for the rest of the evening – the start of the music, any further arrangements for food, such as a late cold buffet, etc.
- Help to keep things running smoothly by making introductions, chatting to guests. Try to look as though you're enjoying every minute; a fixed grin won't fool anyone but try to keep smiling, listen, and watch what's going on around you.
- After the bride and groom have had the first dance, dance the second dance with the chief bridesmaid.
- Throughout the evening, dance with the bride, her mother, the groom's mother and as many female guests as possible.

> ➤ If you have a wife or girlfriend, avoid the possibility of a public row by explaining in advance that all that dancing with other women is part of your duties. And mean it.

- Rescue the bride and groom from those guests who monopolise them so that they can circulate as much as possible.
- Try to encourage people to mingle.

- If the drinks run dry, send out for emergency supplies.
- If anyone has too much to drink, take them out of the main area and try to sober them up with water, coffee and a little food.

> ➤ Don't try to break up groups of people who are obviously enjoying each other's company in an attempt to make them mix – it's better to introduce other people into the group.

- Supervise the decoration of the couple's car, making sure no one causes any damage.
- Make sure the couple's luggage is in the get-away car.
- When the couple are about to leave, make an announcement to let everyone know.
- See the couple to their car and hand over any documentation to the groom – tickets, passports, keys, etc.
- Take charge of the groom's wedding outfit.
- Organise someone to collect any telemessages, telegrams, cards, e-mails and a few mementos such as place cards, flowers, and napkins to give to the newly-weds when they return from honeymoon (this is a good one for the bridesmaids).
- Ensure that nothing is left behind at the reception.
- Help the bride's parents to see the guests safely on their way home.
- Ensure that all guests have transport home.
- Help to clear up.

The best man's data

Use these pages to keep all your information together and be the most efficient best man ever!

Who's who

Role	Name	Address	Telephone	Mobile	E-mail
Bride					
Groom					
Chief bridesmaid					
Bridesmaid					
Bridesmaid					
Flower girl					
Pageboy					
Pageboy					
Chief usher					
Usher					
Usher					
Bride's mother					
Bride's father					

The best man ———————————————————————

Role	Name	Address	Telephone	Mobile	E-mail
Groom's mother					
Groom's father					
Special guests					

Ceremony details

Wedding date	
Wedding time	
Church/register office	
Venue	
Telephone	
Mobile	
Fax	
E-mail	
Restrictions (on confetti, photos or videos)	
Parking facilities	
Possible hold-ups on the route	
Time needed to get to church from home	
Time to leave home	
Time to arrive at church	

Reception details

Contact	
Venue	
Telephone	
Mobile	
Fax	
E-mail	
Parking facilities	
Cloakroom facilities	
Gift display/store facilities	
Microphone facilities	
Bar facilities	
Meal arrangements	
Entertainment arrangements	
Changing room for bride and groom	
Number of guests	
Receiving line	
Seating plan of top table	
Toastmaster's name	
Arrival time	
Time to start meal	
Time for speeches	
Time for bride and groom to leave	
Bar closes	
Time for guests to leave	

Transport

Personalise the data sheet with all the information you need. In some cases – the ushers, for example – you may just have to check that they have made their own arrangements and have the times correct.

Emergency taxi firms	
Car hire firm	
Address	
Telephone	
Fax	
E-mail	
Cars to be provided	
Cost (deposit and final cost)	
Payment dates	

From ... to	For	Organiser	Vehicle	Flowers or ribbons	Driver	Pick-up time	Arrival time
Home to ceremony	Groom and best man	Best man					
Ceremony to reception	Bride and groom	Best man					
	Best man						
	Bridesmaids and pageboys	Bride's family					
	Bride's mother and groom's father	Bride's family					
	Groom's mother and bride's father	Bride's family					
	Chief usher						
	Usher						
	Usher						
	Special guests						
Reception to honeymoon	Bride and groom	Best man					

The best man ————————————————————————

The stag night

Date	
Location	
Final number of guests	
Venue 1	
Address	
Telephone	
Fax	
E-mail	
Booking confirmed	
Venue 2	
Address	
Telephone	
Fax	
E-mail	
Booking confirmed	

Guest	Address	Telephone	Mobile	E-mail	Invited √ Accepted √ √	Transport

The flowers

You should know exactly when and where to collect the flowers, and how many there should be, so that you have them at the church for distribution to the wedding party.

Number of buttonholes	
Number of corsages	
Collect from	
Time to collect	

Chapter 3
The Ushers

The role of an usher at a church wedding is much less formal than it used to be. Ushers used to be essential to escort the bridesmaids, so there were always the same number of ushers as bridesmaids, but nowadays they are there to help out the best man and generally make things run more smoothly. There will usually be about one usher to every 50 or so guests, and there is often a chief usher, who co-ordinates the rest and deputises for the best man if he finds he is meant to be in two places at once.

If you have been asked to act as an usher at a wedding, you are probably a brother or relative of the bride or groom, or a close friend. It's a mark of affection to be asked, and it's an easy job, so just check out what you need to be doing – and enjoy!

What do I have to do?
The duties of the ushers are quite straightforward. This is what you will be expected to do. If there are lots of ushers, the chief usher will co-ordinate everything and share out the jobs between them.
- Escort or guide guests to their seats at the church.
- Distribute order of service sheets.

- Hand out the buttonholes and corsages.
- Escort the bridesmaids throughout the day.
- Make sure all the guests have transport to the reception.
- If the best man is leaving the church for the reception with the rest of the wedding party, the chief usher is responsible for making sure nothing and no one is left behind, so he will be the last to leave.
- Be generally helpful at the reception to make sure everything runs smoothly.

Do I receive an invitation?

The groom or best man should ask you personally to act as an usher, but you will also receive an invitation from the hosts, usually the bride's parents. Don't assume that because it should be obvious that you'll be attending, you needn't reply. Send a **written** reply within three days of receiving the invitation, in the same style of formality as the invitation itself. For example, if the invitation is in the third person ('Mr and Mrs Fred Bloggs request the pleasure ... '), reply in the third person (Mr Brian Smith would like to thank Mr and Mrs Fred Bloggs ... '); remember, you do not sign a note written in the third person. Otherwise a brief and polite note of acceptance is fine ('Thank you very much for your kind invitation to ... I am delighted to accept ... ').

> ➤ You are not expected to give the bride and groom any more special a gift than you would if you were an ordinary wedding guest.

What should I wear?

There will be a dress code for the wedding, fixed by the bride, so the groom or best man will let you know if it's a formal wedding (in which case you are expected to wear a morning suit). If it's less formal, a lounge suit will be appropriate. If it's a formal wedding, the hire of your morning suit should be paid for by the groom's family, but if not, then you will be expected to provide your own suit (you don't have to buy a new one if you already have something appropriate). If it is morning dress, you don't actually have to wear your top hat and gloves; carry them in your left hand, holding the hat by the brim. Whether it is formal or informal, your shoes, socks and all your accessories are your responsibility.

> ☺ Arm yourself with a large umbrella if there's a chance of rain, so you can accompany people from their cars to the church door. Use your discretion when choosing one – avoid advertising a brand of beer, if possible, and remember that, if it's a formal occasion, it should be black.

It's a good idea to have a trying-on session about a week before the wedding to check that you have absolutely everything you need. Don't forget that formal shirts need cufflinks.

Escorting the guests in church

At the church, the bride's family and friends sit on the left and the groom's on the right. The groom and the best man will be sitting on the aisle-end of the right front pew, and the groom's parents sit behind them. The groom's close relatives sit in the next few pews, then the groom's other relatives and friends. The bride's mother sits in the front pew on the left, leaving a space for her husband to join her. Behind her sit the bride's close relatives, then other relatives and friends. Families with babies or young children are best guided to pews at the rear of the church and to seats nearest the aisle so that they can make a hasty exit if necessary.

Make sure you find out if there are any special circumstances, such as divorced parents, and how such couples would like to be seated. Traditionally, if they are not remarried, the parents sit together; if they are remarried, they sit with their partners.

If it's obvious that the number of guests on each side of the church will be very unbalanced, just check with the best man that you can use your discretion in filling the pews evenly.

At a formal wedding, you will be expected to escort guests all the way to their seats. Offer your left arm to a lady; her partner will follow behind. If two ladies arrive together, escort the eldest first. For men, simply accompany them to their seats. For a less formal wedding, you can simply direct guests to the appropriate pews.

> ➤ If you are not used to escorting a lady – and who is? – just remember you offer her your left arm because it leaves your sword arm free to protect her! If you are left-handed, that's tough, I'm afraid, as tradition doesn't cater for you.

The last member of the congregation to arrive should be the bride's mother. The chief usher escorts her to her seat in the front pew on the left. You all then take your seats in the back pew. If anyone arrives late, get up and escort them to a rear pew as quietly as possible.

The order of service sheets

The ushers handing out the order of service sheets should make sure they have enough to give one to each member of the congregation (that's everyone on the guest list). Before the guests start to arrive, place a few on the front pews for the bride, her father, the bridesmaids, pageboys, groom and best man. Then simply hand out the sheets as you escort the guests to their seats. If there are any restrictions at the church, such as no confetti or no photographs in the church – both of which are common – find out and mention them to guests as they arrive.

The buttonholes

Each of the wedding party – that's all the important guests – wears either a buttonhole (for the men) or a corsage (for the women). There should be enough for all the ushers, the groom's parents and the bride's parents. The bride's father should be given his buttonhole beforehand, so that he can be wearing it when he escorts his daughter to the church, and the women will probably want to pin theirs on when they are dressing, but the ushers may distribute the rest at the church.

The transport

After the ceremony, photographs will be taken outside the church, and then the main wedding party will leave for the reception. Be helpful in getting everyone to their cars and make sure no one is without a lift. One of the ushers, usually the chief usher, should be the last the leave and do a final check to ensure that nothing – and no one – has been left behind.

> ➤ If it's a formal wedding, make sure everyone has picked up their top hats and gloves.

The rehearsal and the stag night

There may be a rehearsal of the ceremony a week or so before the wedding. Take the opportunity to check everything and ask any questions.

As one of the principal men, you should also be invited to the stag night, so make sure you write the day in your diary well in advance and clear the following day to recover.

At the reception
Your escort duties don't end at the church; you're expected to accompany the bridesmaids all day! With any luck, this will be more of a pleasure than a chore, but if there are any very young bridesmaids, take your responsibilities seriously and prepare some activities to keep them – and other younger guests – busy during the reception. If possible, arrange for the following to keep them amused (it will be worth the effort if it leaves you a bit of space to get to know the older bridesmaids):

- Videos.
- Games.
- Toys.
- Picture books.
- Colouring books and crayons.

You may be asked to take the guests' coats or offer them drinks when they arrive. It will also be helpful to offer your services handing round drinks or trays of nibbles, helping people to their seats, chatting to guests and generally making sure everything goes well on the day.

The ushers' diary

Six months before
- ❏ Enter the wedding date in your diary.
- ❏ Cancel any other engagements for that date and the preceding couple of days.
- ❏ Chat to the best man about what you are expected to do.
- ❏ Find out what you are expected to wear and who is paying for your outfit if it is hired.

Three months before
- ❏ Consult and return the wedding gift list, buy gift, gift card and wrapping paper.
- ❏ Arrange to meet the wedding party members so you all know who's who.
- ❏ Make sure you know about any restrictions in the church on such things as confetti, photographs, etc.
- ❏ Buy or arrange to hire your outfit and accessories.
- ❏ Buy or borrow a large black umbrella to shelter guests if it rains.
- ❏ Send a written reply to the invitation within three days of receipt (see page 174).
- ❏ Receive from the best man seating plans for church and reception.

One to two weeks before
❑ Attend the stag night.
❑ Attend the rehearsal.
❑ Confirm the arrangements for collecting buttonholes and order of service sheets.
❑ Deliver your gift to the bride at her parents' home.
❑ Prepare some activities to keep the youngsters quietly occupied during the reception.
❑ Have a hair cut.
❑ Collect your outfit if hired. Check you have all the accessories and that everything fits. Polish your shoes and remove any price tags from their soles.

The day before
❑ Clean the wedding cars and check the petrol.
❑ Charge up your mobile phone.
❑ Run through the order of the day so you know what you are doing (see pages 235–41).
❑ Double-check all the arrival times, routes and schedules.

On the day
❑ Collect the order of service sheets, buttonholes and corsages from the best man or bride's mother. Distribute the flowers to the wedding party as appropriate.
❑ Arrive at the church in good time.

After the event

❑ Return outfit if hired.
❑ Send a thank you note to the bride and groom if they have given you a gift.

The ushers on the day

At the ceremony

- You should arrive first at the church about 40 minutes before the ceremony is due to start.
- Switch your mobile phone to **silent**.
- Put in your buttonhole.
- Organise the parking.
- Escort the congregation to their seats.
- Distribute the order of service sheets and place some in the front pews for the wedding party.
- Tactfully remind guests if there are to be no photographs or confetti.
- The chief usher escorts the bride's mother to her seat.
- Take your own seat at the back for the ceremony.
- Join the recessional as the wedding party moves out of church.
- Direct the guests to the photo area and help the photographer to position the guests for the photos.
- Ensure that all guests have transport to the reception.

- Tidy up and make sure nothing is left behind – check all the pews.
- Clean up confetti if asked to do so.
- Leave the church grounds last.

At the reception
- Offer drinks to guests as they arrive.
- Introduce guests to each other.
- Show guests to their seats, particularly any who are elderly or disabled.
- Generally make yourself useful in ensuring that the reception runs smoothly.
- Keep an eye on the bridesmaids, especially the young ones.
- Dance with as many female guests as possible.
- Encourage people to mingle.
- Help the best man to decorate the get-away car.
- Make sure that all guests are taken home safely and that nothing is left behind.

The ushers' data

Who's who

Role	Name	Address	Telephone	Mobile	E-mail
Bride					
Groom					
Best man					
Chief bridesmaid					
Bridesmaid					
Bridesmaid					
Flower girl					
Pageboy					
Pageboy					
Chief usher					
Usher					
Bride's mother					
Bride's father					
Groom's mother					
Groom's father					
Special guests					

Clothes

Menswear supplier, if hired	
Address	
Telephone	
Date of fitting	
Date for collection	
Payment arrangements	
Shoes	
Socks and underwear	
Shirt	
Tie	
Waistcoat	

Things to do

	Date	Time
Collect order of service sheets		
Collect buttonholes and corsages		
Deliver buttonhole to bride's father		
Address		
Deliver corsage to bride's mother		
Address		
Deliver corsage to groom's mother		
Address		

Chapter 4
The Bride's Father

This is your daughter's big day when – as tradition would have it – you are handing over the responsibility for your daughter to her husband. Although the tradition is a relic of the time when she was considered to be a chattel to be passed from one male to another, I'm sure that's not how you see the occasion! If you are not fit to burst with pride now, you will be when you see your daughter in her wedding dress and ready to walk down the aisle.

If, for any reason, the bride's father is unable to give her away, then her uncle or an old friend of the family may be asked to fulfil that role. If that applies to you, your responsibilities for giving the bride away are just the same as if you were her father. You may also be acting as host of the reception, or that may fall to someone else.

In most families, the bride and her mother are the real organisers of the wedding, but the bride's father has a big part to play in all sorts of ways: the planning and organisation, communication between the families, the smooth running of the event, and paying at least some (if not most!) of the bills.

What are my main duties?

You are the host of the wedding, so you will be involved in all aspects of the decision-making and planning – although in reality, much of that will fall to your wife. You give away your daughter to her future husband before the ceremony, and escort the groom's mother from the church. You are the host of the reception, you will say grace if there is no minister present, and you'll have to make a speech.

What happens first?

If the future groom has read his section of this book, he'll ask your permission to marry his daughter – certainly you should be among the first to know that your daughter has got engaged.

It's up to you whether you decide to arrange an engagement party for family and friends. If you do, then you will be the one to announce the good news to the assembled guests and to propose a toast to your daughter and her fiancé, who will thank you and your wife for the party and propose a toast to everyone present.

The next stage is to get together with your daughter and her fiancé and his parents to discuss what kind of wedding they would like, how it is going to be organised, who is going to do what, and who is going to pay for what. Traditionally, the bride's parents host the evening, but the choice of venue is up to you. Invite them round for a meal or just go out for a drink – whatever you feel comfortable with.

Since the bride's father traditionally foots most of the bills, it is very important that you take control of the budget early on. These days, the groom's parents usually contribute to the cost, and often the bride and groom also help towards the expenses, but whatever the circumstances, make sure everyone is clear about their commitments from the beginning otherwise there could be some nasty surprises further down the line.

What am I expected to pay for?

As I said, clarify this from the start. Traditionally, this was a business transaction, so you paid for practically everything. Times have changed, but expectations and arrangements may be different in different families, so it is essential to be clear. The average expenditure on weddings today is over £8,000. Of course, you don't have to spend that much, but it is easy to let things get out of hand if you are not careful.

Don't spend far more than you can afford – it will do nothing to improve the day for you and is more likely to spoil the whole thing. Be realistic from the start. If you have to make compromises, keep in mind what is really important to you. If you want to invite loads of people, keep the food to a finger buffet and make your own taped music. If you would rather have a superb meal, restrict it to the wedding party only and go to the best restaurant you can afford. What really matters is that you are joining with friends and family to celebrate your daughter's big day, not whether you have gone to the expense of printed matchbooks or napkins. You'll find lots more useful information in the groom's chapter, so it's a good idea to read that through as well.

> ☺ There may be some things that your daughter thinks are terribly important but you can't really see why. Remember that she probably feels the same about some things you want and be prepared for a bit of give and take.

As far as the budget is concerned, you are traditionally expected to pay for:

- The engagement party.
- Printing costs, for invitations etc.
- The wedding dress (although often the bride pays for this herself).
- The bridesmaids' and pageboys' outfits.
- Your own outfit.
- Transport, except for the groom and best man to the church.
- The photographer.
- The press announcements.
- The cake.
- Flowers for the church and reception.
- The reception.

The good news is that nowadays the groom and/or the groom's father frequently offer to contribute some of the cost.

The most expensive item will probably be the reception and this is where the groom's side often offers to contribute. The bride and groom may also pay for some things themselves, especially if they are older and established in well-paid jobs. Grandparents or godparents may like to help, too.

✂£ A member of the family or a friend may be happy to make the cake. You may be expected to pay for the ingredients, or they may offer to do the whole thing as their wedding gift.

How on earth do we plan all this?

You'll already know whether your wife and your daughter are going to take charge of the organisation, or whether you'll be ringmaster. This chapter assumes that you'll be taking a supporting role. If that's not the case, get hold of a detailed wedding organiser (see the list on page 250).

☺ Read the list of stress-busting tips on pages 95–6. You might need them for your wife or your daughter. In any event, you may very well want to use them yourself!

Should I take out insurance?

Weddings, as we've already seen, are not cheap and you want to get the best for your financial outlay. Even the most meticulous planning can go wrong, however, and for this reason there is a range of insurance packages on the market. It is worth looking into them to see whether they are appropriate in your case. They can cover:

- Cancellation.
- Non-refundable deposits to suppliers.
- The cost of retaking photos and video.
- Failure of transport.
- Legal costs and expenses.
- Public liability.
- Loss or damage to wedding outfits, gifts, rings, the cake, wedding documents, honeymoon luggage.
- Bad weather.

It's up to you to weigh up the cost of the premiums against the specific risks.

What sort of present do I give?

This is entirely up to you. It's common for the bride's and groom's parents to give the newly-weds a large gift such as furniture, but you may agree that a smaller present is appropriate if you are paying for most of the wedding. In that case, make it something very personal to the happy couple.

What do I wear?

You will have set the style of the wedding at your initial discussions with the bride and groom. It may be formal or informal – or anything in between. Whatever has been decided, all the men in the wedding party – that's the important people – should dress the same.

If it's a formal wedding, that means morning dress, and you'll find everything you need to know about that in the groom's section on pages 71–2. Otherwise, the men most commonly wear smart lounge suits. Make sure you speak with your daughter about the colour schemes she has set and the sort of colours she would like you to wear. If it is a summer wedding, for example, she may like all the principal men to wear light-coloured suits, so you'd look out of place if you chose navy or dark grey. Similarly, find out the colour scheme for the flowers and the bridesmaids' dresses before you buy your tie, shirt, and so on.

☺ If in doubt, ask your daughter. Things like the colour of your waistcoat may seem trivial to you but they will matter to her.

What happens on the stag night?

You'll be invited to join the stag night but the younger generation will expect you to leave early before the party really gets going (sorry!). If you are starting the evening with a meal, then the time when they move on to a pub or club is the ideal moment to back off and leave them to it.

What happens on the day?

For much of the early part of the day, your main role will be one of support. Your home is likely to be in a state of near-uproar as the bride and her mother will both be trying to get ready and everyone's nerves are likely to be under severe strain. It is common practice for the bridesmaids to come to the bride's house to get dressed too and the best man is likely to arrive to collect items such as buttonholes for the men and the order of service sheets. You may be called upon to drive people to and from the hairdresser, to fetch and carry clothes, to take delivery of flowers and probably to provide endless cups of tea (or something stronger).

Eventually, everyone will leave for the church and there will be just two people remaining in the house – you and your daughter. In films, the bride's father makes a short, emotional speech at this point, telling his daughter how much he loves her. ('Ever since you were a little girl and I sat you on my knee . . . ') Even if this is not your style, you will probably want to spend a few minutes talking, and reassuring her if she is nervous. It is always possible that she may be the one trying to calm your nerves. Whatever is said, make it a moment to treasure.

> ➤ Make sure you are ready to leave well before the car arrives – your daughter is traditionally allowed to be late but she won't forgive you if you are the one who holds everything up because you can't find your shoes.

What do I do at the ceremony?

When you arrive at the church, you and the bride will probably pose for a few photographs together before you go in. Then you take her left arm on your right and escort her up the aisle. When the minister asks, 'Who gives this woman to be married to this man?', you step forward and pass your daughter's hand into that of the minister. You then take a step back and the ceremony continues. After the ceremony, prayers, hymns and address, you offer your arm to the groom's mother and escort her into the vestry. You may be asked to sign the register as a witness (the bride and groom should have decided who is to do this beforehand). You then escort the groom's mother from the church. After the photographs, the bride and groom will leave for the reception, followed by you with the groom's mother, the bride's mother with the groom's father, and the bridesmaids and best man.

What about the reception?

You are the host of the reception, so you act accordingly. The bride and groom, both sets of parents and the chief bridesmaid and best man should all line up to welcome the guests. When the meal is announced, you take your place at the top table.

Chief bridesmaid	Groom's father	Bride's mother	Groom	Bride	Bride's father	Groom's mother	Best man

If the minister is present, he or she should be asked to say grace before the meal; otherwise you should say grace. Keep it to something simple and short, as it should be memorised, not read. Here are a few examples.

'For what we are about to receive, may the Lord make us truly thankful.'

'Bless, O Lord, this food for our use and us to Thy service.'

'Thank you, Lord, for this food before us, for the love of our families and for the love of – (bride's name) and – (groom's name) on their wedding day.'

'Bless this food, O Lord, as You bless – (bride's name) and – (groom's name) on this their special day.'

After the meal, comes the speeches, and you will propose the toast to the bride and groom. Since this is the part most men dread above everything else, we've given it a special chapter (see pages 217–34), which includes everything you need.

After the speeches and the cake-cutting, the tables will be cleared away for the next phase of the celebrations to begin.

The bride and groom start the dancing, then about halfway through the dance, you take the floor with the groom's mother. After that, it's just like any other party – so enjoy it!

When do the bride and groom leave?

Most couples want to stay at the party for as long as possible. When they are about to go, the best man should announce their departure and ask the guests to make two lines – one for the men and one for the women – leading to the door. Take your place nearest the door. The bride and groom say their thanks and goodbye to all their guests – the groom going down one side and the bride down the other – until they reach the door and leave on their honeymoon.

The party may go on after that, or it may now start to wind down. If you want people to stay and continue the celebrations, it's a good idea to say so, or your guests may feel that they should take this as their cue to leave.

I'm divorced from the bride's mother – how does this change things?

This is not an unusual situation but I'm afraid there is no fixed solution – it will depend on the circumstances and individuals involved. The crucial factor is that you discuss it with your daughter first, to find out how she would like the arrangements to be made, then talk it through with the rest of the family. Your daughter may like you to give her away, act as host for the reception and make the father-of-the-bride speech, as usual. If her mother's new partner has had a great deal to do with bringing her up, she may want you to share the fatherly roles between yourself and her stepfather. It is up to you to discuss with your ex-wife how (or if) any costs are to be shared.

☺ However you feel about sharing fatherly roles, try to keep in mind that this is your daughter's day, so you must make every effort to compromise, wherever necessary, to make sure it is a happy one.

The bride's father's diary

Six months before
❑ Set the wedding budget and agree financial responsibilities with your daughter, her fiancé and his parents.
❑ Enter the wedding date in your diary.
❑ Cancel any other engagements for that date and for the preceding couple of days.
❑ Arrange the engagement party.

Three months before
❑ Meet wedding party members so you all know who's who.
❑ Buy a wedding gift.
❑ Buy or arrange the hire of your outfit.

❏ Write your speech.
❏ Ask the minister to say grace if he or she is going to attend the reception, otherwise decide what you are going to say.

One week before

❏ Make sure that your insurance policy covers everything you need (remember that wedding gifts at the reception should be covered against theft, for example).
❏ Attend the stag night.
❏ Check your outfit, polish your shoes and make sure you remove any price tags.
❏ Attend the church rehearsal and rehearsal get-together and give your gift.
❏ Pay the bills.
❏ Check through the list of what to do on the day so you know what to expect.

On the day

❏ Leave a message on your home answerphone giving a few contact numbers, for example the reception venue and the best man's mobile number, in case guests get lost en route to the venues.
❏ Take the telemessages, telegrams, cards and e-mails to pass on to the best man at the reception.
❏ Switch your mobile phone to **silent**.

The bride's father on the day

At the ceremony

- You should arrive last, with your daughter.
- Lead the procession (by escorting your daughter followed by her attendants) down the aisle to the chancel steps with your daughter on your right arm.
- Take a step back but remain at the chancel steps for the time being.
- When requested (*'Who giveth this woman ... ?'*), take the bride's right hand and give it to the minister.
- Step back to join your wife in the first pew on your left for the remainder of the service.
- Escort the groom's mother to the vestry for the signing of the register.
- Sign the register if you have been asked to act as one of the two witnesses.
- Escort the groom's mother out of the church.
- After the photographs, the bride and groom leave first for the reception, followed by the best man and the bridesmaids. You then leave with the groom's mother.

At the reception

- When you arrive at the reception, join your wife to form the start of the receiving line to greet the guests.

- Once everyone is seated for the meal, you say grace if there's no minister present.
- Indicate to the waiters and waitresses when you want them to start serving.
- After the last course, the toastmaster or best man will introduce you. You then make the first speech and propose the first toast.
- The bride and groom will start the dancing. Halfway through the first dance, you invite the groom's mother to join you on the dance floor. For the rest of the party, you can dance with as many guests as you wish. If dancing isn't really your thing, then try to meet and talk to as many of your guests as possible.
- When the bride and groom are ready to depart, arrange the leave-taking line with the help of the best man and the ushers.
- You should be one of the last to leave, after all the guests.

> ➤ Check with the best man that he is going to take the wedding gifts, the remains of the cake and mementoes such as napkins, place cards, and keepsake register. If not, you should do this. Whatever you do, don't assume he's doing it – he might be making the same assumption . . .

The bride's father's data

Who's who

Role	Name	Address	Telephone	Mobile	E-mail
Bride					
Groom					
Best man					
Chief bridesmaid					
Bridesmaid					
Bridesmaid					
Flower girl					
Pageboy					
Pageboy					
Chief usher					
Usher					
Usher					
Groom's mother					
Groom's father					
Special guests					

Clothes

Menswear supplier, if hired	
Address	
Telephone	
Date of fitting	
Date for collection	
Payment arrangements	
Shoes	
Socks and underwear	
Shirt	
Tie	
Waistcoat	

Budget sheets

Use the groom's budget sheets on pages 119–24 as these include all the items you need to account for.

Chapter 5
The Groom's Father

Congratulations! You have really hit the jackpot. Not only are you going to be one of the proudest people there on the day you celebrate your son's wedding, but you traditionally have very little responsibility for the proceedings, so you can really relax and enjoy yourself.

What are my main duties?
You are a guest at the wedding – a very important one, of course, but a guest nonetheless.

Traditionally, almost everything was arranged and paid for by the bride's family. Nowadays, however, things are rather different and the groom's parents usually contribute financially to the wedding. This also means that they are more involved in setting the style and making the arrangements. Try to meet the bride's parents as early as possible so you can discuss the whole thing and get to know each other before the big day. You can take that opportunity to offer your help and support in whatever way you prefer. They will usually arrange the meeting but if it is not suggested, perhaps you could invite them to a meal or an informal evening at your house.

You and your wife will be expected to supply a list of the guests to be invited from your side of the family. You'll have to pay for your own wedding clothes, whether bought or hired, and of course, you're expected to buy the bride and groom a special wedding gift. You'll be invited to attend the wedding rehearsal and the stag night. On the wedding day, you will follow the bride and groom into the vestry and may be asked to sign the register as a witness. You'll then escort the bride's mother from the church and to the reception. At the reception, you will have a seat at the top table for the meal. Once the bride and groom have started the dancing, you'll join the dance about halfway through with the bride's mother.

> ➤ If you are sociable and welcoming to all the guests, this is where you can make a real contribution, by helping to make the party go with a swing.

How does it all begin?
You should be among the first to know about your son's engagement. If the bride's family arranges an engagement party, you'll be invited to join the celebrations, or you might like to offer to host an engagement party yourself. If it's a formal occasion, the bride's parents will announce the happy news and toast the couple, and your son will respond with a few words of thanks. You can then say a few words if you wish.

Once that is over, this is a good time to organise a meeting with the bride's parents and the bride and groom so that you can talk through the wedding arrangements and get everything under way. You could invite them to lunch, dinner, or just casual evening drinks. It only needs to be formal if you want it to be, although in that case your wife is supposed to write the first letter. It's probably nicer to set an informal and relaxed tone from the start, so a phone call to say how happy you are at the news and to make contact is absolutely fine.

What should I offer to pay for?

One of the things to discuss at that meeting is money. This is always a tricky subject, and there are no set rules here, so it is important that you make the first move and offer your support, making it quite clear whether you want that to be financial or practical or both. Decide before the meeting how you would most like to make your contribution. You can take the initiative by saying you will pay for something specific, or you can offer a set amount of money, or perhaps undertake to organise certain aspects of the wedding – or you can do all three!

☺ Since, traditionally, the bills are down to the bride's father, it is best if you come forward first to say what you will pay for. He may think it would seem rude to ask and anyway, he may feel too embarrassed to do so.

Do make sure you are tactful; make it clear that you are making the offers because you want to be involved in celebrating your son's wedding, not because you don't think the bride's family can afford anything good enough for your son!

> ☺ If your family has an heirloom worn by successive generations of brides, offer it to the bride – but don't feel hurt if she declines.

What about the guest list?

Once it has been decided how many people you can invite overall, each family normally invites half, although if one family is substantially larger than the other, you may have to agree a proportionate split of numbers. Make a list with your wife and son of your relatives and friends and give that to the bride's mother. Include any children that you want to be invited – they may be small but they still add to the numbers and you may have to compromise if there are too many.

Why do I get an invitation?

Since the bride's parents are the hosts of the occasion, they'll send you and your wife an invitation. This may seem a little unnecessary, but don't assume that you needn't reply. Send a written reply within three days of receipt in the same style as the invitation. For example, if it is a formal invitation, written in the third person, reply in the third person – you don't need to sign it.

What should I wear?

The bride and groom will have decided whether they want a formal or informal wedding, and all the principal men must be guided by their decision. If the outfits are to be hired, you'll have to liaise with the groom about suppliers and fittings, and make sure your outfit is collected and then returned after the wedding. If you are required to wear a lounge suit, then you should go shopping in good time to buy something suitable. In either case, you are responsible for all the costs, including shoes, tie and accessories.

Make sure you ask the bride about her colour scheme for the wedding. If all the men are in dark suits, you'll stick out like a sore thumb if you go for beige linen. The overall style and colour does matter. It's also worth asking about colours for ties, waistcoats and so on. The bride may want you to complement the bridesmaids and the flowers. That might not make much sense to you but, trust me, the photos will look much better!

☺ Read the list of stress-busting tips on pages 95–6. Even if you don't get stressed by big occasions, your wife may, and anyway it's a good time to make sure you are working on your marriage, too!

What else do I need to do?
Your plans should be the same as for any major event to which you have been invited. Do a bit of planning and check up as many items as possible well in advance so you can be relaxed and enjoy the occasion to the full.

☺ If some of the guests are travelling to the wedding from some distance away, perhaps you could offer overnight accommodation at your own home or that of friends, or suggest local bed-and-breakfasts or hotels. If you are arranging hotel accommodation, do make clear whether you are paying or not.

- Get all your clothes sorted out early, have a trying-on session and make sure everything fits.
- Decide how you are going to get to the ceremony, to the reception, and home from the reception. Check timing, road conditions, possible hold-ups and parking arrangements. Your wife will not forgive you if you are late at any stage of the proceedings.
- Make sure you can leave your car at the reception venue and book a taxi home if you intend to have a few drinks. Better still, use a reliable taxi service for all your trips.
- Check on your timing. The arrival time at the church is crucial.

- Think about your wedding gift and choose something appropriate.
- Run through the list of what happens on the day (see pages 235–41) so you know what to expect.

Do I go to the stag night? And what's a rehearsal for?
You'll be invited to join the stag night the week before the wedding, but the younger generation will probably expect you to leave early before the party really gets going (don't worry, the bride's father will get the same treatment). You might like to join them for a meal, then leave when they move on to a club or pub.

☺ You could offer to act as taxi service later in the evening if you are not drinking earlier on.

About a week before the wedding, you and your wife may be invited to the rehearsal at the church to run through the ceremony with the rest of the wedding party. It's a good opportunity to iron out any final queries, check on times, and offer to undertake any last-minute jobs. There's often a party or a meal afterwards, which may be a good time to give your wedding present to your son and his future wife, although you may want to choose a more personal occasion.

☺ You could offer to host the post-rehearsal meal if you feel the bride's parents have been doing most of the work for the big day.

What am I supposed to do at the ceremony and the reception?

You should arrive at the church in good time and take your seat in the second pew on the right. After the marriage ceremony, when the bride and groom go to the vestry to sign the register, offer your left arm to the bride's mother and escort her to the vestry. You may be asked to sign the register as a witness (this should have been decided in advance). You then leave the church with the bride's mother, following your wife and the bride's father.

If there are no ushers at the wedding, you could volunteer to help out the best man, collecting the buttonholes to take to the church, guiding guests to their seats at the ceremony, giving out order of service sheets, and so on. Remember that this will require you to be at the church much earlier, so your wife may want you to arrange separate transport for her.

After the photographs, you leave for the reception with the bride's mother, and join the receiving line to welcome the guests. You will take your place at the top table (see opposite) when the meal is announced.

Chief bridesmaid	Groom's father	Bride's mother	Groom	Bride	Bride's father	Groom's mother	Best man

You are in the fortunate position of not having to make a speech, but if you would like to say a few words, tell the groom or the best man in advance so he can make sure you are announced in the right order.

The bride and groom will have the first dance then, towards the end of the song, you invite the bride's mother on to the dance floor. After that – enjoy! You can, of course, help out by making sure people mix, and bringing any lonely souls into conversation. Even if you just dance with as many people as possible, you will be making your contribution to ensuring that the whole thing goes with a swing.

I'm divorced from the groom's mother – how does this change things?

Just be guided by whatever you think will make your son's big day as relaxed and happy as possible. Discuss it with him if you can and try to remember that on this occasion his feelings are more important than yours. If he wants you to bury the hatchet and sit with his mother, do it – and smile too. Generally speaking, you sit in the church with your new partner, if you have one, and your ex-wife does the same. Seating at the top table will be arranged to allow new partners to be involved, if appropriate. As far as costs are concerned, you and your ex-wife have to decide whether you will both contribute.

The groom's father's diary

Six months before
❏ Meet your son, his fiancée and her parents to discuss wedding plans.
❏ Make a guest list for your side of the family.
❏ Enter the wedding date in your diary.
❏ Cancel any other engagements for that date and the preceding couple of days.
❏ Attend the engagement party.

Three months before
❏ Meet all the wedding party members so you know who's who.
❏ Buy your wedding gift.
❏ Buy or arrange to hire your outfit and accessories.
❏ Send a written reply to the invitation within three days of receipt.

One month before
❏ Write and practise a speech if you wish.
❏ Finalise all your transport arrangements.

One week before
❏ Attend the stag night.
❏ Collect your hired outfit.

- ❏ Check all your clothes, polish your shoes and remove any price tags or labels.
- ❏ Attend the church rehearsal and rehearsal get-together, and give your wedding gift.
- ❏ Ask the bride's parents if they need any practical help at the last moment.

The day before
- ❏ Wash your car and make sure it is filled with petrol.
- ❏ Run through what you are supposed to do.
- ❏ Check your timings and taxi bookings.
- ❏ Charge up your mobile phone.
- ❏ Have a couple of emergency taxi numbers programmed into your mobile just in case.

On the day
Be ready in good time to get to the church.
Now check through the list of what to expect on the day (see pages 235–41).

After the wedding
- ❏ Send a thank you letter to the bride's parents for arranging, organising, and paying for the wedding, if appropriate.
- ❏ Write a thank you letter to your daughter-in-law and son if they bought you a gift.
- ❏ Return your suit if hired.

The groom's father on the day

At the ceremony
- Arrive early.
- Switch your mobile phone to **silent**.
- Pose for photographs with the groom, the best man and the ushers.
- Sit with your wife in the second pew from the front on the right behind the groom and best man.
- After the marriage, offer your left arm to the bride's mother and join the wedding party procession to sign the register.
- Sign the register as one of the two witnesses, if requested.
- Offer your arm to the bride's mother again and follow your wife and the bride's father out of church.
- After the photographs, leave for the reception with the bride's mother, after the bride and groom.

At the reception
- Join the receiving line after the bride's parents to greet guests as they arrive.
- Take your place at the top table when the meal is announced.
- Enjoy your day!

The groom's father's data

Who's who

Role	Name	Address	Telephone	Mobile	E-mail
Bride					
Groom					
Best man					
Chief bridesmaid					
Bridesmaid					
Bridesmaid					
Flower girl					
Pageboy					
Pageboy					
Chief usher					
Usher					
Usher					
Bride's mother					
Bride's father					
Special guests					

The groom's father

Clothes

Menswear supplier, if hired	
Address	
Telephone	
Date of fitting	
Date for collection	
Payment arrangements	
Shoes	
Socks and underwear	
Shirt	
Tie	
Waistcoat	

Chapter 6
The Speeches

Most men dread their wedding speech more than anything else. Presumably on the basis that if they ignore it long enough it might just go away, they also tend to leave preparing it till the last minute! This is a Seriously Bad Move. If you are one of the principal men, you will be expected to make a speech, so the sooner you get used to the idea, the better. With a bit of planning and forethought, the whole thing becomes much less terrifying. You **can** do it – and you can do it **well**. Take a few moments to think about what's really involved. If you can approach it with confidence, you'll carry it off with style. Try to persuade yourself that it really is not such a big deal. After all:

- You have a supportive audience who want to have a good time and want you to succeed.
- A wedding speech should only be a few minutes long anyway.
- You don't have to be a stand-up comic.
- Wishing your daughter/son/best mate every happiness in a sincere way is really all that is needed.

Read this chapter of essentials to set you on the right track, and if you feel you need some more help, get hold of *Mitch Murray's One-liners for Weddings* (also published by Foulsham), for some more in-depth help from an expert. You can also look at the list of books on speech-making listed on page 250 – they even provide you with sample speeches to adapt to your circumstances.

Who makes the speeches and when?

The speeches take place after the last course of the meal. If there is a toastmaster, he will introduce each speaker in turn. If not, the best man usually fulfils this role. In either case, make sure you all know the order in which you are speaking. This is the traditional order.

The bride's father: He makes his speech on behalf of himself and his wife to introduce the bride to the groom's family. He then proposes the toast to the happiness of the bride and groom.

The groom: He thanks his new father-in-law on behalf of himself and his wife, thanks his parents for their support and for the wedding, expresses his happiness on the occasion of his marriage and his pleasure at seeing so many guests. He proposes the toast to the health of the bridesmaids.

The best man: He replies on behalf of the bridesmaids, usually paying some judicious compliments, and introduces the groom to the bride's family. He also reads out any telegrams or telemessages. He then tells the guests what will happen during the remainder of the celebrations and announces the cake-cutting.

These days, the bride often chooses to say a few words herself, and she can do so after the groom, but she is perhaps better waiting until after the messages, which usually makes for a better flow of speeches. There's no set pattern to a bride's speech as it is a relatively new phenomenon, but it is best just to make sure you are not all repeating the same things.

Everyone stands when a toast is proposed, except the people being toasted.

> ➤ Although traditional, it's not compulsory for any principal man to make a speech, so if you really feel that you would ruin the day, speak to the groom and the best man and the speech can either be omitted or someone else can say a few words on your behalf. This is perfectly acceptable, but don't leave it to the last minute to back out.

What about speeches at second marriages?

That's really up to the hosts and the bride and groom, so make the decision, or find out what has been decided, depending on your role. Whatever you say, you must **not** refer to any previous relationship. At a formal second wedding, the bride's father will not actually be giving her away, so he may not be expected to make a speech. Whatever is right for your wedding is the right choice.

How long should the speeches be?

The best speeches are often the short ones. Four minutes is ample, five is the maximum and at small informal receptions of lunch or drinks they can be even shorter – that's somewhere around 500 words, if you're counting. A wedding audience expects only a few sincere and perhaps amusing words and then the toasts; they're probably more interested in having a good time. A long, meandering and nervous speech will only embarrass everyone.

How do I prepare my speech?

Be organised – take it step by step.

- Start early. The sooner you have something roughed out, the more confident you'll feel about the whole thing.
- Think of the type of reception and the level of formality that is expected – you'd write a different speech for an informal gathering of friends than for a formal dinner for 150.

- Check if there are any special people you have to thank or any sensitive issues to steer clear of: divorced parents, recent bereavements, and so on.
- Find out who else is speaking and make sure your ideas and jokes don't overlap.
- Jot down facts and ideas as you think of them and keep them together somewhere safe.
- Create an outline for your speech: one paragraph of thanks, one paragraph of anecdotes, one paragraph proposing the toast, for example. Give it a beginning, a middle and an end.
- Make a first draft, not worrying too much about length, then keep going through it until you feel comfortable with it and it's about the right length. Use short sentences; don't include any long words that might trip you up; don't worry too much about the rules of grammar (imagine you're talking to friends, not giving a lecture); make sure it flows and is easy to deliver.
- Edit your speech by deleting repetitions and unnecessary words; if it's too short, you could add a suitable quotation, joke or anecdote as long as it fits with what you're saying and doesn't sound like padding!
- Carry it with you so that you can amend it from time to time when things occur to you. Add, replace and delete information, until you are happy with it.
- Prepare a few notes or headings that you can use as a reminder to keep you on track, but try to have the whole

thing so well memorised that you can deliver it without hesitating. Highlight key words and phrases.

- Alternatively, use numbered index cards as memory-joggers, punch a hole in one corner and slip them on to a treasury tag to keep them together and in sequence.
- Practise it in front of a mirror. Time how long it takes.

What can't I say?

A formal wedding will demand a more formal speech, but however informal it is, there are some things you should avoid.

- Swearing – even a 'damn' or 'blast' can offend some people; everything you say should be suitable for everyone present, including the minister or your elderly maiden aunt.
- Being rude – any sort of vulgarity or bad taste will be out of place and you should never say anything that could embarrass or offend in any way.
- Embarrassing anyone present – particularly either the bride or the groom or any member of their families. Even if you think you are being funny, this is never a good idea. Don't refer to any previous marriage or relationships of either of the happy couple and don't mention any family arguments, divorces, etc. And don't even try to make jokes at the expense of anyone present or anyone they know.
- Referring to anything sad – this is not the moment to bring to mind the bride's favourite uncle who has recently died.
- Using slang – it detracts from the sense of occasion.

What can I say?

You are all there to celebrate a happy occasion but there's a reason for each of the speeches, as I've outlined above. Make sure you know why you are making your speech, which people you have to thank or mention, and whether you are proposing a toast, then the rest should follow naturally. The list below contains a few ideas on how it should go.

- Start with: 'Ladies and gentlemen'. However, if it's a formal wedding and there are special guests, perhaps people with titles, then you should acknowledge them first: 'My Lords, ladies and gentlemen'. (No wonder you're nervous!)

- If you are responding to a toast, thank the proposer.

- Relate an amusing quotation, joke or anecdote about the bride or groom. Aim for smiles rather than belly laughs. Beware of telling jokes if you're not the greatest comic, however. There's nothing worse than a joke that falls flat.

- Tell a short story that shows the bride or groom's best qualities – this should go down well with the aunties – look for the nodding heads or approving murmurs ('Aah'!)

- Use one-liners – these are often safer and more effective than long jokes and funny anecdotes.

- If you must tell a joke, make it a gentle one about marriage.

- Telling a joke at your own expense is another safe option.

- Finish by proposing your toast.

Should I learn my speech?

Think about the options and decide which is best for you. You are aiming to combine delivering a structured speech that you have crafted and thought about, with a level of flexibility. You want to say the right things in the right order, but you want it to sound natural.

Reciting from memory is fairly inflexible. It tends to sound unnatural and leaves no room to slot in any unexpected events of the day. If you are nervous and forget what comes next, it could throw you completely. However, if you are able to treat it as a bit of acting, it might suit you.

Reading word-for-word from a script can sound a bit flat. You'll also be looking down at your script and that tends to disengage you from your audience.

The method used by many professional speakers is to learn the main points of the speech by heart and use cue cards as memory-joggers, and it certainly seems to produce the best results. The advantages are that you have your speech planned and know it well, you don't have to worry about forgetting anything as you can refer to your cards if necessary, and you have the scope to improvise with last-minute additions that can really bring a speech to life.

What about rehearsing?

Rehearsing is a definite must, and it's a good idea to do it in front of a mirror (a full-length one, preferably, so that you can see how you stand). You'll find out which bits work and which bits don't, how long the speech will be, where you need to pause for laughter, and so on. It will also help you with your delivery – watch out for yourself fiddling with change in your pocket, making weird gestures or saying 'Um ... er' before each sentence.

You might want to try out the speech in front of an audience. Pick one or two people who you know will make constructive comments and ask them to give you their honest reaction and help you make improvements.

➢ If you have a video recorder, make a tape of your performance and watch it so you can get the effect of the speech from the audience's point of view.

What about presentation?

What you say is important – and so is **how** you say it. Think about how you are going to stand, what you are going to do with your hands, and how you are going to project your speech.

➢ Go to the loo before the speeches start!

Find out whether there will be a microphone. If there is, check its position, then leave it alone. Remember not to shout. If there isn't one, you'll have to speak loudly enough to be heard. Project your voice to the back of the room but don't shout. If you're worried about getting the volume right, you could start on a light-hearted note by saying, 'Good afternoon, ladies and gentlemen. Can you all hear me because I'm sure you've been waiting all afternoon for my speech and I wouldn't want you to miss anything!'

> Stay off the alcohol until after your speech, or just have one for a bit of Dutch courage. If you have too much, you may think you sound good, but the chances are that no one else will agree.

Here are a few more pointers to making your speech a success.

- You'll probably be standing at a table with your chair behind you. Make sure you have enough room so you don't knock into it and topple backwards.
- Have your notes or cards on the table in front of you so that you can see them. Put on your spectacles if you need them (this is no time for vanity or pretending you can do without), and have a glass of water ready, plus your wine glass charged for the toasts.

- Pause, take a deep breath and make a start: 'Good afternoon, ladies and gentlemen ...'
- Speak clearly so the audience can hear what you are saying; don't mumble or run your words together.
- Speak a little more slowly than normal; don't rush, however much you want to get it over.
- Use your natural accent; don't try to put on a posh voice.
- Stand still, don't sway or shuffle. Stand up, don't slouch.
- Don't put your hands in your pockets, fiddle with change, scratch yourself or fidget. If you need something to do with your hands, hold your cards and quietly turn them over as you go through the speech.
- Look just above the heads of your audience so they know you are talking to all of them. Look at a specific person if you are talking about them or proposing a toast to them. Don't gaze at the table, the floor or the ceiling.
- Glance quickly down at your notes from time to time, to reassure yourself that your cards are in the right place if you need them.
- If you dry up, take a deep breath, glance at your notes and pick up where you left off. If things start to go wrong, smile, say 'Sorry', then carry on.
- Try to avoid saying 'Um ... er ... like ... '.
- Smile and don't forget to breathe!

> ➤ If you smile, it actually makes you **feel** happier. So it's worth trying, when your nerves are getting the better of you.

- If your audience starts getting noisy – with laughter or applause, we hope – wait for it to subside before you start again.
- Ignore camera flashes and video cameras.
- Pick up your glass when you propose the toast.

☺ The best man could add sparkle and comedy to his speech by including a few visual aids, such as appropriate poster-sized photo cards of the groom, perhaps as a baby or a young boy, or winning an award or a medal (but do avoid bath-time shots!).

I'm so nervous!

Even people who are accustomed to speaking in public get nervous, so you are bound to feel a few stomach twinges. Knowing that you are well prepared is the key. If you have written and practised a good speech, there's really nothing to worry about.

- If you know you will be nervous, write BREATHE on a crib card and place it on the table in front of you. If you feel yourself talking too fast, stop when you can, take a sip of water, breathe and start again, slowly.

- If you know you are likely to fidget, decide in advance what you are going to do with your hands.
- If you think you are likely to forget your speech, write it down and make sure you glance down occasionally so you are always in the right place on your sheet.
- Highlight or colour-code the headings in your speech to help you find the right place.
- If all else fails, thank the previous speaker for their comments, make the appropriate toast and sit down.

The bride's father's speech

It's traditional for you to propose the toast to the bride and groom. If you are not the father, but are making this speech on behalf of the bride's father, obviously you change the wording according to your relationship to the bride. These are the main elements that are usually included.

- Praise your daughter and say how proud you and your wife are, perhaps including an anecdote to illustrate her character.
- Congratulate the groom and welcome him to your family.
- Show your confidence in the couple's future together.
- Wish them a long and happy life, perhaps offering some advice from experience.
- Thank anyone who helped to organise the wedding.
- Announce the toast to the bride and groom, wait while everyone stands up, then make the toast.

Suggested introductions to the toast: 'Please stand and raise your glasses to the happy couple.'

'So, ladies and gentlemen, will you please stand and raise your glasses.'

'Friends, I ask you to stand and drink a toast.'

(Pause for everyone to stand.)

Suggested wording for the toast: 'Here's health and happiness to – (bride's name) and – (groom's name). May they live happily ever after.'

'To the luckiest man alive and his beautiful wife. To – (groom's name) and – (bride's name).'

'Wishing – (bride's name) and – (groom's name) long life, perfect health and happiness. To – (bride's name) and – (groom's name).'

'To the health, happiness and prosperity of the newlyweds. To – (bride's name) and – (groom's name).'

'To the bride and groom – may we all be invited to your golden wedding celebrations. To – (bride's name) and – (groom's name).'

If there are children in the relationship, you may like to include them. For example: 'To the long life and continued happiness of the newly-weds and their young son. To – (bride's name), – (groom's name) and – (son's name).'

The groom's speech

You reply to the toast on behalf of your wife and yourself. Your response is the one with the least scope for wit, as your primary task is to thank everyone involved in organising the wedding.

- Thank your father-in-law for his comments and his toast.
- Say how happy you are, how lucky you are to have such a beautiful wife, how lovely she looks and so on.
- Reassure the audience that you intend to take good care of her and keep her happy.
- Express your pleasure at becoming part of your wife's family.
- Thank the hosts for a wonderful wedding and everyone involved for their generosity.
- Thank your own parents for their support and for putting up with you thus far!
- Thank everyone for their gifts and for attending the wedding, mentioning specific people if necessary.
- Thank the attendants for their support and hard work, for looking beautiful, or whatever is appropriate to their age and role.
- Ask everyone to stand to toast the bridesmaids, and pause while they do so. Then make your toast to the bridesmaids by name.

Suggested introduction and toasts: 'Please stand and join me in a toast.' (Pause for everyone to stand.)

'I ask you then to drink a toast to these beautiful girls (name them) who attended and supported – (bride's name) on and before this our big day. Ladies and gentlemen – the bridesmaids.'

'– (name the chief bridesmaid), my wife's chief bridesmaid, has been a great sport and support to – (bride's name), with all her hard work today and in the many weeks of preparation. Let us all raise our glasses to her for her help and for looking so beautiful. Ladies and gentlemen, to – (name her).'

'I know that you'll join me in thanking – (name the bridesmaids), the beautiful bridesmaids, and – (name the pageboys), the handsome pageboys, for their participation today. The bridesmaids and pageboys.'

The best man's speech

If there's no formal toastmaster, you'll take on his role. Ask for silence and introduce each speaker. Check before you start that everyone has a charged glass – there's nothing worse than seeing a guest raise an empty glass and mime drinking a toast! Rise and smile at the guests, lightly tapping a glass for attention. If this doesn't work, say clearly, 'Ladies and gentlemen, your attention please!' saying, for example, 'Ladies and gentlemen, the father of the bride', or whoever it may be.

The best man replies on behalf of the bridesmaids, and your speech is usually the one with the lightest tone.

- Thank the groom on behalf of the bridesmaids for his toast and add a few complimentary remarks of your own.
- Thank the groom on behalf of the bridesmaids for their gifts.
- Say what a pleasure it's been carrying out your duties.
- Thank anyone who has helped you do a good job.
- Thank anyone who has been especially helpful to the bride if not already thanked by the groom.
- Elaborate on the groom's background, saying how long you have known him, what the bride's family can expect. Make it light-hearted and affectionate.
- Congratulate the bride and groom and offer some thoughts on their future.
- Read any telemessages, cards and e-mails from absent friends. If there are several with the same message, just read out the message, then the list of senders.
- Toast absent friends if appropriate.
- Toast the host and hostess.
- Toast the bride's and groom's future happiness.
- Tell everyone what is happening for the rest of the celebration, what time the bride and groom will leave and when the reception will end.
- Announce the cutting of the cake.

Suggested introduction and toasts: 'Please stand and join me in a toast.' (Pause for everyone to stand.)

'On behalf of the bridesmaids and pageboys, thank you, and let me add my own good wishes to the lucky couple. To – (bride's name) and – (groom's name).'

'We wish – (bride's name) and – (groom's name) the very best in their life together and long may it continue. To – (bride's name) and – (groom's name).'

'To – (bride's name) and – (groom's name). It's the first day of the rest of your life together. To – (bride's name) and – (groom's name).'

The bride's speech

Since there's no set pattern to this, the bride can say what she likes! She usually offers her personal thanks to her parents for bringing her up and for hosting such a wonderful day. She thanks the guests for sharing the occasion with them, and looks forward to a long and happy life with her new husband. If she makes a toast, it will be to her husband, and she usually drinks the toast alone.

Suggested toasts: 'To my husband. May you share everything with me – including the housework.'

'To my husband. Here's to a long and happy life together.'

Chapter 7
The Order of the Day

This is a full run-through of everything that happens on the big day. The more specific things that apply to individual members of the wedding party are listed in their own chapters. This chapter is intended to give you a complete overview of events. If it's useful, cross out anything that doesn't apply to you personally, fill in the right times and anything extra you want to include. If you know what to expect, you'll feel confident and relaxed and able to enjoy the day to the full.

Time	Order of events
–2 hours (at least!)	Everyone checks their final arrangements, ticks off everything that should be done and gets dressed in time for the ceremony.
	The best man picks up the order of service sheets, buttonholes and corsages and takes them to the church or gives them to the chief usher to take.
	The best man should be sure he has the ring(s), documentation (ceremony fees and certificates), honeymoon documents (travel tickets, passports, hotel reservations), emergency telephone numbers, speech and mobile phone.

The order of the day

Time	Order of events
–45 minutes	The ushers arrive at the church early and distribute the order of service sheets, buttonholes and corsages.
–30 minutes	The best man picks up the groom and arrives at the church.
	Photos are taken at the bride's house.
	Photos are taken of the principal men at the church.
	The best man and the groom take their seats.
	The groom's parents arrive at the church.
	Minister, organist and bell-ringers arrive. The organist plays quietly and the bells are rung.
	The best man hands over banns certificate from the groom's church and pays fees.
–20 minutes	The guests arrive and the ushers escort them to their seats.
	The bride's mother arrives with the bridesmaids.
	The bridesmaids wait in the church porch.
Zero hour	The bride should arrive on time with her father.
	The photographer takes some shots of the bride's arrival.
	The chief usher escorts the bride's mother to her seat.
	The ushers take their seats in the rear pews.
	The music for the procession starts and the groom and the best man move forward to stand at the chancel steps. The congregation stands up.

Time	Order of events
	The minister may either lead the procession, or wait at the chancel steps as the bride and her father, with the bridesmaids, walk to the chancel steps.
The service	The bride's father leads the bride to the groom's left, then takes a step back.
	The bride turns for the chief bridesmaid to lift her veil, and take her bouquet and gloves. If there's no bridesmaid, the bride's father takes the bouquet and gloves and hands them to the bride's mother who returns them to the bride later in the vestry for the recessional.
	The attendants may remain standing behind the bride, but younger ones are usually seated in the front pews.
	The service begins with a greeting, then the minister talks about the significance of marriage.
	The congregation will be asked whether anyone knows a reason why the marriage should not take place.
	The minister asks the couple to declare their intention to marry and asks the groom: 'Wilt thou have this woman to be thy wedded wife, to live together according to God's holy law in the state of matrimony? Wilt thou love her, comfort her, honour and keep her in sickness and in health and, forsaking all others, keep thee only unto her, so long as ye both shall live? He answers: 'I will' (NOT 'I do'!).
	The minister asks a similar question of the bride and she responds accordingly.

The order of the day

Time	Order of events
	The minister asks: 'Who giveth this woman to be married to this man?' The bride's father steps forward, takes his daughter's right hand and presents it palm-down to the minister. The minister places it in the groom's right hand.
	The minister guides the couple through their vows.
	The minister offers the best man the open prayer book. He places the rings on the book and the minister blesses the bride's ring and offers it to the groom. The groom places it on the third finger of the bride's left hand and repeats his promise after the minister. If the groom has a ring, the bride puts it on his hand now.
	The bride's father and the best man step back.
	The minister pronounces the couple 'man and wife' and the groom may kiss the bride.
	The bride and groom kneel at the chancel steps and the congregation kneels for prayers and the blessing.
	The minister leads the couple to the altar for prayers.
	The service continues with hymns, prayers and a psalm.
	The minister gives the blessing.
	The bride takes the groom's left arm and follows the minister to the vestry. They are followed in order by the best man (who picks up the groom's hat and gloves) and the chief bridesmaid (with the bouquets), the attendants, the bride's father with the groom's mother, and the groom's father with the bride's mother.

Time	Order of events
	The bride (using her maiden name) and groom sign the register, as does the minister and two adult witnesses. The minister may allow a photograph. The minister hands the groom the marriage certificate.
	Meanwhile, in church, the organist will be playing and a soloist may be singing.
	The chief bridesmaid returns the bride's bouquet and gloves.
	The groom offers his left arm to the bride and they lead the recessional out of the church, followed by the wedding party in the same order as they entered. A photograph is usually allowed in the church at this time.
	The bells are rung in celebration.
	The congregation follows the party outside.
	The photographs are taken.
	The bride and groom leave for the reception, escorted to their car by the best man.
	The best man escorts the bride's mother and the groom's father, then the groom's mother and bride's father to their cars.
	The best man escorts the bridesmaids and attendants to their cars, then leaves with them for the reception.
	The guests follow.
	The ushers check that no one and nothing has been left behind, then leave for the reception.

Time	Order of events
The reception	At a very formal reception, a professional toastmaster will announce the guests as they approach the receiving line. Guests place any gifts on a table adjacent to the line.
	The bride's parents, groom's parents, bride, groom, best man and chief bridesmaid line up to receive the guests. They take the opportunity to introduce members of the family. (Note, to avoid nose-jarring clashes, the rule is to offer your left cheek for a polite kiss.)
	The guests are offered a drink and they circulate until everyone has arrived.
	The chief bridesmaid and the best man take charge of any gifts and place them to one side until later.
	The best man collects the telemessages and cards from the bride's father and checks that everyone has their speeches.
	The chief bridesmaid asks guests to sign the keepsake register.
	The toastmaster or best man asks people to take their seats for the meal. If the meal is a buffet, they should make it clear whether guests should collect their meal before sitting down, or take their seats and go to the serving table when asked. The ushers help guide people to their seats.
	The minister or the bride's father says grace before the meal.
	After the meal, the toastmaster or best man makes sure everyone's glasses are charged for the toasts.
	He introduces the speakers and they make their speeches and toasts.

Time	Order of events
	The bride and groom cut the cake.
	There is usually a lull while the meal is cleared away.
	The bride and groom lead the dancing with a slow dance. The bride's father joins in with the groom's mother, and the groom's father with the bride's mother, then the best man and chief bridesmaid.
	That's the signal to party!
	The best man and chief bridesmaid remind the couple when it is time to change, and help them if necessary. They take charge of the wedding outfits. The best man hands over the honeymoon documents.
	The guests make two lines – one male and one female – towards the door, with the wedding party members nearest the door, and the bride and groom proceed between the lines, saying their farewells.
	The bride throws her bouquet backwards over her shoulder towards the assembled bridesmaids.
	The party continues as long as the host and hostess wish.
	When all the guests have left, the best man should check that nothing has been left behind.

Further Information

Books

There's a list of useful books for all the members of the wedding party on page 250.

Magazines

Brides and Setting Up Home, The Condé Nast Publications Ltd, Vogue House, 2 Hanover Square, London W15 1JU. Tel: 0207 499 9080

Wedding and Home, IPC Media Ltd, King's Reach Tower, Stamford Street, London SE1 9LS. Tel: 0207 261 7470

You and Your Wedding, Nat Mags and Specialist Media, Silver House, 31–35 Beak Street, London W1F 9DL. Tel: 0207 437 2998

Help on the net

There's almost too much information available on the web, and it takes time to separate the good from the useless. Here are just a few useful sites to get you started.

General information

www.confetti.co.uk Designed to make your wedding experience enjoyable and stress-free, this site aims to meet the needs of everyone involved in the wedding.

www.weddings-and-brides.co.uk Products and services for weddings and honeymoons.

www.weddingbells.com The site of the similarly named American magazine published twice a year, with many of the articles being free for you to browse on the web site. Information for the best man and the parents of the bride and groom, guidance on stag nights, many sample speeches and information about the wedding ceremony.

www.weddingchannel.com Aimed at helping both men and women through the process of planning a wedding and starting a new home.

www.weddingguide.co.uk Advice to wedding planners, including details of stag activities.

Church of England weddings

www.cofe.anglican.org/lifechanges/wedding Details of the legal requirements and fees.

Register office weddings

www.registerofficeweddings.com Use this site to locate the register office closest to you and find all the information you need on procedures, including how to book, how much notice is required, how much it will cost, and so on.

Weddings abroad
www.weddings-abroad.com The company arranges over 4,000 weddings each year for couples wishing to marry outside their country of residence and boasts some of the most beautiful and exquisite places to marry in the world.

Speeches
www.hitched.co.uk Sections for everyone involved and an enviable selection of suitable jokes and tips for speeches. You can even buy stag and hen night 'accessories' in its online shop.

Hindu weddings
www.lalwani.demon.co.uk/sonney/wedding If you're participating in a Hindu marriage ceremony and you are unfamiliar with the arrangements, find out what to expect.

Jewish weddings
www.jewish.org.pl/english/edu/JewFAQ/marriage.htm Part of a huge site giving information on all aspects of Judaism, which has a comprehensive guide to Jewish weddings.

Honeymoons
www.webwedding.co.uk An impressive database of over 10,000 wedding suppliers – for everything from rings to honeymoons – with some special offers and competitions as well. There are also links to online wedding stores.

Information about married life

www.2-in-2-1.com An American site about shaping and maintaining your marriage as well as the usual wedding services. The marriage clinic covers all sorts of marital problems and issues and also has links to many other marriage research sites.

www.marriagecare.org.uk Information on marriage in the UK, marriage preparation classes run by the Catholic church, advice on how to maintain a healthy, happy marriage and details of courses in your area.

www.marriageencounter.freeserve.co.uk Offered by the Anglican church, this site helps married couples to get the most out of their marriage and their commitment to one another, and learn to improve their relationship. It's open to all married couples, whatever their faith, and consists of a weekend learning break in which you can explore and share your feelings, hopes, joys, fears and disappointments while learning to improve communication and deepen your relationship. It's not recommended as an alternative to counselling for couples with serious problems.

Useful Addresses

Organisations

Church of England
Enquiry Centre,
General Synod of the Church
of England,
Church House,
Greatsmith Street,
London SW1P 3NZ
Tel: 020 7898 1000

Church of Scotland
Department of
Communication,
121 George Street,
Edinburgh EH2 4YN
Tel: 0131 225 5722

Scottish Episcopal Church
21 Grosvenor Crescent,
Edinburgh EH12 5EE
Tel: 0131 225 6357

Scottish Executive
St Andrew House,
Regent Road,
Edinburgh EH1 3DG
Tel: 0131 556 8400

**Representative Body of the
Church of Ireland**
Church of Ireland House,
Church Avenue, Rathmines,
Dublin 6
Tel: 0035 3149 78422

Methodist Church
Press Office, 25 Marylebone
Road, London NW1 5JR
Tel: 020 7486 5502

Baptist Union
Baptist House,
129 Broadway, Didcot,
Oxfordshire OX11 8RT
Tel: 01235 517700

Religious Society of Friends (Quakers)
Friends House,
173–177 Euston Road,
London NW1 2BJ
Tel: 020 7387 3601

United Reformed Church
86 Tavistock Place, London
WC1H 9RT
Tel: 020 7916 2020
And
Church House,
340 Cathedral Street,
Glasgow G1 2BQ
Tel: 0141 332 7667

General Register Office for England and Wales
Marriages Section,
Room C201, Smedley Hydro,
Trafalgar Road, Southport,
PR8 2HH
Tel: 0151 471 4803

Office for National Statistics
PO Box 56, Southport
PR8 2GL
Directory of registered
premises costs about £5 (2001)
Tel: 0151 471 4817

General Register Office for Scotland
New Register House,
3 West Register Street,
Edinburgh EH1 3YT
Tel: 0131 334 0380

General Register Office for Northern Ireland
Oxford House,
49–55 Chichester Street,
Belfast BT1 4HH
Tel: 02890 252000

Presbyterian Church in Ireland
Church House,
Fisherwick Place,
Belfast BT1 6DW
Tel: 02890 322284

General Register Office for the Irish Republic
Joyce House,
8–11 Lombard Street East,
Dublin 2
Tel: 0035 3167 11863

General Register Office for the Isle of Man
The Civil Registry,
Deemster's Walk, Bucks Road,
Douglas,
Isle of Man IM1 3AR
Tel: 01624 685265

Registrar General for Guernsey
The Greffe, Royal Court House, St Peter Port,
Guernsey GY1 2PB
Tel: 01481 725277

Superintendent Registrar for Jersey
10 Royal Square, St Helier,
Jersey JE2 4WA
Tel: 01534 502335

Registrar of the Court of Faculties
1 The Sanctuary,
Westminster,
London SW1P 3JT
Tel: 020 7222 5381
(for special licences)

Catholic Marriage Care
Clitherow House,
1 Blythe Mews,
Blythe Road,
London W14 0NW
Tel: 020 7371 1341

Jewish Marriage Council
23 Ravenhurst Avenue,
London NW4 4EE
Tel: 020 8203 6311

British Humanist Association
47 Theobalds Road,
London WC1X 8SP
Tel: 020 7430 0908

Shopping
**British Antique Dealers'
Association**
20 Rutland Gate, Kingsbridge,
London SW7 1BD
Tel: 020 7589 4128

Housing Corporation
149 Tottenham Court Road,
London W1P 0BN
Tel: 020 7393 2000

**Association of British Travel
Agents (ABTA)**
68–71 Newman Street,
London W1T 3AH
Tel: 020 7637 2444

**National Wedding
Information Services**
Astra House, West Road,
Templefield, Harlow,
Essex CM20 2BN
Tel: Freephone 0500 009027
or 01992 576461

Musicians' Union
60–62 Clapham Road,
London SW9 0JJ
Tel: 020 7582 5566

Passport Office
Clive House, 70 Petty France,
London SW1H 9HD
Tel: 0870 521 0410

**National Association of
Toastmasters**
4 Dukes Orchard, Bexley,
Kent DA5 2DU
Tel: 01322 554342

Other Foulsham Titles

Foulsham Essentials
Your Brilliant Wedding Speech 0-572-02762-1

Foulsham's Wedding Collection
The Complete Wedding Organiser and Record 0-572-02338-3
Your Wedding File 0-572-02427-4
Your Wedding Planner 0-572-02415-0
Wedding Etiquette 0-572-02409-6
The Best Best Man 0-572-02339-1
The Best Man's Organiser 0-572-02303-0

Foulsham's Speeches and Toasts
Mitch Murray's One-Liners for Weddings 0-572-01896-7
Mitch Murray's One-Liners for Speeches on Special Occasions
0-572-02388-X
Mitch Murray's Handbook for the Terrified Speaker
0-572-02459-2
Wedding Speeches and Toasts 0-572-02410-X
Wedding Speeches 0-572-01781-2

Foulsham's Family Finance
Step by Step to Buying and Selling Your Home 0-572-02690-0

Index

Index